READING SCRIPTURE DEEPLY

MILLENNIALS TAKE A FRESH LOOK AT THE BIBLE.

Edited by Richard S. Hess

And

E. Randolph Richards

Reading Scripture Deeply

Publishing Information

Publisher: International Reference Library for Biblical Research

Title: Reading Scripture Deeply

Subtitle: Millennials take a fresh look at the bible.

List of Contributors

Joseph R. Dodson
Ouachita Baptist University, Arkadelphia, AR
Ralph K. Hawkins
Averett University, Danville, VA
Richard S. Hess
Denver Seminary, Littleton, CO
Michael D. Matlock
Asbury Theological Seminary, Wilmore, KY
Caryn A. Reeder
Westmont College, Santa Barbara, CA
E. Randolph Richards
Palm Beach Atlantic University, West Palm Beach, FL
Beth M. Stovell
Ambrose Seminary, Calgary, Alberta, Canada

Copyright: 2015 International Reference Library for Biblical Research
ISBN-13: 978-1514853603
ISBN-10: 1514853604

Reading Scripture Deeply

PREFACE

The book arose from a conference hosted at Tyndale House, University of Cambridge, by the gracious financial generosity of the Ellis Foundation for Biblical Research, through the International Reference Library for Biblical Research (IRLBR). Nominations for participants were solicited from the Institute for Biblical Research. We warmly thank both groups for their support.

The goal of the conference was to build warm collegial relationships between rising evangelical scholars with the hope of forming lifelong friendships based upon mutual respect and shared mission. The initial vision came from E. Earle Ellis who greatly prized the importance of evangelical scholars building relationships in person, living in community, using the skills and talents given to them by the Lord for the service of the Church.

The success of the conference was aided by the leadership of two more experienced scholars, Rick Hess and Randy Richards, who guided discussions and modeled collegiality, and who themselves were blessed by joining in the community. The challenges of organizing, hosting and facilitating such an ambitious endeavor would not have succeeded without the able leadership of Daniel Fredericks, himself a skilled Old Testament scholar, who added his own expertise and leadership to the discussion tables. We also want to thank Mr. Jesse Grenz, a promising young scholar, for the arduous task of incorporating edits from seven different people and then standardizing them into a coherent document.

Contributing to this volume required sacrificing time and energy. We want to thank our institutions and our families for allowing it.

May the Church find this volume helpful as we all seek to read Scripture deeply.

E. Randolph Richards

TABLE OF CONTENTS

ABBREVIATIONS

BBR	Bulletin for Biblical Research
ch.	chapter
EBR	Encyclopedia of Bible and Religion
e.g.	for example
ibid.	the same
m. Sanh.	Mishnah, Sanhedrin tractate.
n.	note
NICNT	New International Commentary on the New Testament
NIV	New International Version
NRSV	New Revised Standard Version
NT	New Testament
OT	Old Testament
Pr Man	Prayer of Manasseh
Spec. Laws	Philo, On the Special Laws
v.	verse
VTSup	Vetus Testamentum Supplement Series
vv.	verses

READING SCRIPTURE DEEPLY

MILLENNIALS TAKE A FRESH LOOK AT THE BIBLE.

Reading Scripture Deeply

CHAPTER 1

INTRODUCTION

Richard S. Hess

In Acts 8:26-39 we read the story of the Ethiopian eunuch who longed for someone to come and assist him in understanding the ancient writings of Scripture. The Holy Spirit sent him the apostle Philip whose explanation led to the eunuch's conversion to Christianity. In June of 2013 eight scholars convened at Tyndale House, Cambridge, England, to devote a week to the discussion of how to interpret the Bible. Our vision in the book before us is to come alongside and join in the reading and interpretation of Scripture, so that we can all gain a better knowledge of its meaning and represent that meaning in our lives and relationships.[1]

The fruit of our discussions from that summer appear in the following chapters. Five of our number devoted themselves to the production of two chapters each. These deal with a range of subjects related to biblical interpretation in the twenty-first century. The result is a multi-dimensional introduction to the subject for the Bible reader who wishes to know how to approach some of the vexing problems of the biblical text and, more importantly, simply to read the Bible in such a way as to gather the most from this experience. So we begin with some basic ideas about what it means when we read the Bible (Chapter 2). Chapters 3-7 discuss major themes and people whom the reader will encounter repeatedly throughout the Bible. We ask questions about how they should be read and provide some basic direction. Chapters 8-10 examine some of

---

[1] We understand Scripture to include the 39 books of the Protestant Old Testament and the 27 books of the Christian New Testament. The New International Version of the Bible will be used unless otherwise noted.

3

the sensitive areas of biblical interpretation that sometimes divide Christians and at other times raise questions about the nature of God. Chapter 11 provides a summary of some of the methods and approaches that the book has considered, and that the reader can use to enhance and deepen their Bible reading.

With the goal of gaining a better knowledge of the Bible's meaning and message, Joseph R. Dodson provides some "Vantage Points" to understand how Scripture interprets itself. He examines examples of how the New Testament cites the Old Testament and thus the Bible "reads itself." In this manner we come to appreciate how the New Testament explores the text of the Old and how it invites us to read beyond the immediate citation to see the larger context of both passages.

Dodson considers allegories and thus anticipates the use of this term by the other authors. An allegory is a connection between a person, description, or event and a concept or larger point that it represents. Writers often understand an allegory as an extended metaphor. While a metaphor is a single item that represents something else, an allegory traces this in a larger picture, often using multiple symbols. So, in Ecclesiastes 12, vv. 1-8 form an allegory of old age. Verse 1 makes this identification. However, the first line of v. 3, "when the keepers of the house tremble," forms a metaphor or single word picture or metaphor. Many interpreters understand this as the loosening of one's teeth that often accompanies old age.

Dodson looks at grace, sin, and death in Romans 5 and James 1 in order to show that manner in which these theological ideas become personified as people engaged in various human activities. He concludes his survey of approaches by considering typologies, those individuals or events that in some manner foreshadow future people and events by describing parallel circumstances and the meanings that develop from them. Here Dodson considers figures such as Adam and Noah, and events surrounding Babel and Pentecost. Surveying all three approaches, we begin to see the vistas of interpretation that lay open to the biblical authors and become available to us as we interpret the biblical text.

Ralph Hawkins considers the biblical story of "Redeeming God's People" as the vehicle that later Scriptural authors developed and interpreted. He demonstrates the heritage that the book of Joshua draws upon when it alludes to the Pentateuch. This occurs especially in the promise to Abram of Genesis 12:1-3 that is repeated and developed in Genesis. Hawkins finds examples of land, nationhood, blessings, and curses in Joshua that reflect this promise.

Hawkins considers the influence of the twin themes of the exodus and conquest in the remaining books of the Bible, as well. Drawing upon these great acts of God, the Psalms, the prophets, and the New Testament writers develop them and find in them a foreshadowing of the life and work of Jesus. His discussion on the epistle to the Hebrews is especially enlightening. Hawkins finds the promised rest of ch. 4 not yet realized, yet looking forward to the full redemption of Jesus Christ as the promised Messiah.

Michael Matlock introduces us to the wisdom of the Jewish writers between the Old and New Testaments. On the one hand, they draw together and develop themes from the Old Testament. On the other hand, they anticipate how the New Testament will understand this material. He studies the figure of King Manasseh in 2 Kings and 2 Chronicles, observing how the Chronicler develops more of this figure's character. The latter biblical author records a repentance and response to God as appearing late in the life of Manasseh. The intertestamental author of the Prayer of Manasseh moves further by envisioning the prayer of the king that signaled his turn toward God. It also takes themes from other great penitential prayers of the Old Testament and incorporates them. Finally, Matlock considers Jesus' parables and the manner in which they focus on aspects of repentance. With this method Matlock provides a deeper understanding of repentance toward God and the ways in which we can participate in receiving divine grace and forgiveness.

Beth Stovell teaches us to listen to God's prophets in order to receive his full counsel. She looks at the image of the vine in Isaiah. There the prophet indicts Israel for its sin. He uses the vine to represent the nation. Behind this lies vine imagery found in Psalm 80 and elsewhere.

There as well it appears to describe the nation of Israel as fruitful in the land where it was "planted." Yet it also portrays God's people under his judgment. Stovell then traces this imagery into the New Testament. She considers the allegory of the vine that Jesus describes in John 15. Jesus replaces Israel in the sign of the vine. Yet Jesus also identifies himself with Israel. Again and again, in terms of creation, idolatry, and the relationship of Christians to the Old Testament and Israel, Stovell demonstrates the insights that the vineyards of Isaiah 5 and John 15 provide.

Joseph R. Dodson returns to consider the typological element in the portrait of Jesus. If his earlier chapter looked at types such as Babel and Pentecost, here the emphasis is on people. In the gospel of Matthew Jesus fulfills the type as a new Moses who brings his teaching with authority. In Mark's gospel Jesus also embodies a new Elijah. In this typology he performs similar miracles of raising children from the dead and of multiplying loaves and fishes. In doing so, however, he exceeds the wonder working of Elijah in the stories of 1 and 2 Kings. For the gospel of John Jesus becomes the fulfillment of the type of Wisdom personified, as found in the Old Testament wisdom literature and even more in the intertestamental Wisdom of Solomon. Jesus also foreshadows a figure such as Stephen in his testimony and his experience of suffering death at the hands of religious leaders. Dodson concludes by examining the genealogy of Matthew 1 and the women portrayed there. Despite their backgrounds and experiences, they become part of the line of Jesus and anticipate (as types) the experience of Mary. She also suffered dishonor at the hands of those who did not believe the virgin birth of Jesus. However, she was honored more than all her predecessors. These explorations take us farther along the road to understand types.

In her first contribution in this book Caryn Reeder explores the significance of Old Testament typologies as used in the New Testament to describe false teachers in the early church. Unlike previous examples of types, these identify figures and groups that the reader should avoid, rather than emulate. Thus Balaam, the archetypal false prophet, who led Israel into sexual and religious sin (Numbers 31:16), becomes the model of the false teachers at Pergamum who led Christians into sin (Rev 2:14, 20-23). The church at Thyatira may face similar deceptions (Rev 2:20-23). Here, however, the author of Revelation, John, uses the Canaanite-born queen of Israel, Jezebel, as the model of those who lead others in idolatry and sexual sin. 2 Peter 2 uses types drawn from the "sons of God" who sinned in Genesis 6:1-4, as elaborated in the intertestamental book of 1 Enoch, and the whole generation of violence that God judged with the flood (also in Genesis 6). These anticipate the judgment of the wicked false teachers of the apostle's day. Balaan also appears here (2 Peter 2:10-19).

If the picture shifts from the nature of the false teaching (as in Revelation) to the character of the false teachers (so 2 Peter), that shift continues in the letters of 2 Corinthians and 1 Timothy. Here the emphasis lies with the people who are influenced by these teachers and their response. In 2 Corinthians 11:3-4 Paul warns the church in Corinth to resist false teaching, unlike Eve who was deceived by the serpent. Reeder observes the manner in which the supports a positive typology of the Church as the new Eve, just as elsewhere Paul sees Christ as the new Adam. This allows for some important insights into the text of 1 Timothy 2:11-15, where Eve also appears.

Caryn Reeder writes the first of two essays that examine a single text from the Old Testament and provide us with detail as to how it moves into the New Testament and finds interpretation there. She traces the literal interpretation of the rebellious son of Deuteronomy 21:18-21 through references to rebellion in Proverbs, discussions of this attitude in Philo and Josephus (with Herod's sons), and on into Rabbinic laws and discussion. The rebellious son also becomes a typology where the son becomes Israel. The prophets repeatedly discuss this as it also appears in the New Testament, whether the Christians of Corinth in 1 Corinthians 5 or the prodigal son of Luke 15. In this manner Reeder demonstrates the ways in which the variety of intertextual and typological readings provide a background for the interpretation of Scripture.

A single example of a single focus occurs in the chapter by Beth Stovell. Stovell returns to instruct us in one of the great Christian word pictures of the Bible: the Suffering Servant of Isaiah 40-55 and that of the gospels. Stovell examines the four Servant Songs in Isaiah in their context. She focuses on Isaiah 53 and the manner in which it echoes the earlier

Servant Songs. Thus the Servant becomes rejected, a payment for sins, brought to death, and one who sits with kings and redeems the nations of the world. She also considers the referent of these Songs as either an individual or a people (i.e., Israel). In so doing, she anticipates the development of the Suffering Servant in Zechariah, in the gospels, and finally in relation to the Philip's explanation to the Ethiopian eunuch in Acts 8. The picture emerges to provide an existential understanding of our own suffering in the context of the Suffering Servant. Alongside the Servant Jesus' vicarious suffering for our sins, as Christians we also see the redemptive value of passing through that suffering and knowing that we are not alone nor is the experience without value.

Hawkins returns to his study of Joshua and the Conquest accounts that generations have identified there as justification for destruction of others. Here, however, he focuses on the Amalekites of Exodus 17 who are not mentioned in Joshua but found first in Exodus 17:8-16. Hawkins traces this interpretation as a justification for violence against one's enemies. Christians have wielded the sword and found justification for it with the Crusades, religious wars, and wars of colonial conquest. Hawkins sees this violence as unacceptable and suggests and alternative set of principles. In so doing he identifies more with Augustine than with Jerome. Thus Christians should not find in these Old Testament accounts any justification for war. Hawkins draws his points from exegesis (the Amalekites do not appear in the New Testament), theology (Jesus re-interpreted these battles as spiritual warfare where he called Christians to a battle that was not concerned with inflicting physical violence), and eschatology (the wars of Revelation), among others. The result forms a good starting point for discussion of the violence of God and for a discussion of these texts. Further, it provides a counter-point (and perhaps an application) to Stovell's preceding chapter on the Suffering Servant.

Michael Matlock provides the final study with a survey of many basic principles for the interpretation of Scripture. The concern to make notes and to trace significant repetitions of terms, phrases, and themes remains perhaps the most valuable starting point for the study of a biblical text. The raising of questions also serves as a valuable means of connection with the text and its interpretation. Matlock discusses the importance of context at multiple levels. This all provides background to the identification of quotations, typologies, and allegories. Matlock reviews an example of allegory in Augustine's interpretation of the Good Samaritan, noting its weaknesses.

In his conclusion, Randy Richards ties these observations together and challenges us as Bible readers to move forward with a deepening of our own skills and approaches to reading the Bible. The perspective of the book provides the Bible reader with new tools with which to encounter the Bible and to uncover something of its grand message of creation, sin, redemption, and consummation. This message is the great story of the Bible and of what our lives can experience as we learn to read deeply into the Word of God.

CHAPTER 2

WHY SHOULD WE CARE ABOUT ALLEGORIES AND SUCH?

Joseph R. Dodson

My family once trekked to the north rim of the Grand Canyon. When we arrived, we sprang from the vehicle and raced onto a giant rock jutting into the sky. We marveled at this breathtaking wonder of the world. Our eyes darted around trying to fathom it all. Each time we caught a fascinating feature we had not previously noticed. I then realized that one of my sons had stopped beside our vehicle. I urged him to join us. He could see *so much more* from our vantage point. To my dismay, however, he was content to enjoy the view from the car. His vista was still spectacular, but there were multitudes of other astounding sights he missed because he was satisfied to remain where he was.

For many years I stood stunned before Scripture and attempted to grasp the landscape of God's love. After a while, however, I began to take the view for granted. I had seen the same passages from the same perspective for so long that I got bored. Consequently, Scripture no longer inspired my love for the Lord as it once did. But then I ventured farther from the car. I started to discover how investigating passages from different angles revealed great and unsearchable truths I had never seen before. These fresh perspectives led to a renewed appreciation of the Bible and restored vitality in my relationship with Christ. These new insights also reinvigorated my ministry. Due to the constant demands of a pastor, I had gotten to the point where I was so eager to arrive at the contemporary application of a passage that I bypassed a more comprehensive understanding of it. As a result, my sermon applications were often anemic, abstract, hackneyed or just plain wrong.

11

The authors of this book believe that a fuller appreciation of Scripture helps foster a deeper walk with Christ and a revived vigor in ministry. Therefore, in this book, we want to lead you out farther. We will invite you to some less traveled terrain that has provided us with new perspectives by which to understand and treasure the Bible all the more. We will focus on three vantages: citations, allegories and typologies.

> The authors of this book believe that a fuller appreciation of Scripture helps foster a deeper walk with Christ and a revived vigor in ministry.

Citations

The first step away from the car is moving beyond reading Scripture to explore how Scripture reads itself—that is, how biblical authors cite and allude to previous passages. When we investigate how and why the biblical authors use quotations we discover extraordinary insights. But just as peering into the depths of a canyon can paralyze a person, so can all the questions that rise up once we peek beyond the surface of the text. For instance, there are times when biblical authors quote passages without informing us who or what they are citing. Do they assume we will recognize the passages on our own? (How many quotations would we miss without the help of bold fonts and cross-reference notes in our modern study Bibles?) Further, what is the significance of the different ways authors introduce citations—such as "as it is written" in comparison to "as Scripture foresaw…and announced;"[2] or as "Isaiah cries out"[3] in contrast to as "the Holy Spirit says"?[4]

Moreover, do the authors cite the respective passages exactly or do they tweak the verses (e.g., leaving out words or changing their order)? If so, what are the implications of these modifications? There are also questions involving context. For instance, is the quotation of a single verse meant to evoke the surrounding verses, chapters, or narrative? Or, does

---

[2] Galatians 3:8.
[3] Romans 9:27.
[4] Hebrews 3:7.

the citation have little to do with the original situation? Along these lines, does the cited verse originally mean what the current author says it means? And why does the author quote Scripture in the first place—to illustrate an argument, to support a thesis, to marginalize the verse as outdated, or for some other reason?[5]

As I said, all these questions can cause one's head to spin. So before we get too dizzy, let us come back from the edge and focus on a few examples to give you an idea of the type of insights you will find in the pursuing chapters. Although biblical authors often cite passages without any modification, the following examples demonstrate the tendency of New Testament authors to cite Old Testament passages and reinterpret them in light of the gospel.

Psalm 22 and Mark 15

Mark only records one sentence that Jesus spoke on the cross: and he does so in Aramaic—*"Eloi, Eloi, lema sabachthani;* (i.e. "My God, My God, why have you forsaken me")? Thereby, Mark provides a clue that this is more than a mere cry of desolation. Rather, on closer inspection, we discover a citation of Psalm 22:1. Going back to the Psalm, we find striking similarities between David's words and the circumstances around Jesus' cross. Below are some highlights.

---

[5] For more on Paul's citations of OT verses, see Joseph Dodson, "The Voices of Scripture: Citations and Personifications in Paul." *BBR* 20.3 (2010), pp. 419-32.

13

Psalms 22	Mark 15
"let the Lord rescue him. since he delights in him." (vv. 6b-8)	And at three in the afternoon Jesus cried out in a loud voice, *"Eloi, Eloi, lema sabachthani?* "My God, My God, why have you forsaken me" " (v. 33-34) Those who passed by hurled insults at him, shaking their heads …In the same way the chief priests and the teachers of the law mocked him among themselves. "He saved others," they said, "but he can't save himself! Let this Messiah, this king of Israel, come down now from the cross, that we may see and believe." Those crucified with him also heaped insults on him. (vv. 29-32)
My God, My God, why have you forsaken me? (v. 1)	
I am scorned by everyone, despised by the people. All who see me mock me;	
they hurl insults, shaking their heads.	
"He trusts in the Lord," they say,	
Let him deliver him,	
Dogs surround me,	
a pack of villains encircles me;	
they pierce my hands and my feet	
All my bones are on display;	And they crucified him. Dividing up his clothes, they cast lots to see what each would get. (v. 24)
people stare and gloat over me.	
They divide my clothes among them and cast lots for my garment. (vv. 14-18)	

Mark wants us to recognize this connection with the Psalm. But his use of the Psalm raises some questions. For instance, why does Mark reverse the order? Did you notice that? The Psalmist gives (A) the cry of desolation, then (B) the insult by the crowds, and then (C) the account of the villains piercing his extremities and casting lots for his clothes. Mark, on the other hand, begins with (C) the crucifixion and the casting of lots to set up (B) the insults and (A) the final climax—the cry of desolation.

Moreover, does the evangelist use David's words only to underline Jesus' suffering or also to highlight the hope of the situation? It light of the empty tomb, it would be appropriate if Mark intended for us to understand the end of Jesus' life with respect to the end of the Psalm, which concludes in triumph—not despair.

[God] has not despised or scorned
the suffering of the afflicted one;
he has not hidden his face from him
but has listened to his cry for help.

> Does the evangelist use David's words only to underline Jesus' suffering or also to highlight the hope of the situation?

All the ends of the earth
will remember and turn to the Lord,
and all the families of the nations
will bow down before him,
for dominion belongs to the Lord
and he rules over the nations. (Psalm 22:24, 27-28, NIV)

Psalm 2 and Acts 4

In response to suffering, the church in Acts 4 also cites and reinterprets the Psalms. As she lifts her voice in prayer, the church quotes Psalm 2. "You spoke by the Holy Spirit through the mouth of your servant, our father David:

> Why do the nations rage and the peoples plot in vain?
> The kings of the earth rise up and the rulers band together against the Lord and against his anointed one. (Ps 2:1-2/Acts 4:25-26)

Indeed Herod and Pontius Pilate met together with the Gentiles and the people of Israel in this city to conspire against your holy servant Jesus, whom you anointed.

They did what your power and will had decided beforehand should happen. Now, Lord, consider their threats and enable your servants to speak your word with great boldness. (Acts 4:27-29)

Although the church acknowledges David as the speaker, she marginalizes him as a mouthpiece and ignores his original historical context (i.e., the events surrounding David as a pre-exilic king of Israel). Rather, her prayer explains that the plot of the nations, peoples, and kings in Psalm 2 points to the partnership between Pilate and Herod, the Gentiles and Jews, as they raged together against the Lord Jesus Christ.

Luke likely intends for us to follow the church's lead and connect the rest of the dots between Psalm 2 and Acts 4. We can read between the lines to see God scoffing at those who stand against his Son—the anointed one whom, on the holy mountain, the Lord has established as king (Ps 2:4-6). Moreover, perhaps Luke expect us to notice the similarity between the thesis of his work in Acts 1:8 with God's promise to his Son in Psalm 2:8: "I will make the nations your inheritance, the ends of the earth your possession." Maybe the evangelist even wants us to recognize the beleaguered church as praying for boldness because she knows how the Psalm ends: "Blessed are they who take refuge in the Lord" (2:12).

Habakkuk 2:4 and Romans 1:17

Paul also cites and reinterprets Old Testament passages in light of Jesus Christ. Although Habakkuk and Paul both consider faith crucial for the followers of God,[6] Habakkuk expresses this in a context where he is straining his eyes to see beyond the shadows of the impending exile. Consequently, the prophet pens Habakkuk 2:4 to stress a steadfast trust in God in the face of incredible suffering. In Romans 1:17, however, Paul considers the prophet's words from the other side of the gloom, where faith stands illuminated by the gospel.

---

[6] Douglas Moo, *Romans* (NICNT; Grand Rapids: Eerdmans, 1996), 78.

But what exactly does Paul intend to highlight through the words of this minor prophet—the person of Jesus Christ or the means of salvation? For example, is the apostle reading a messianic promise into Habakkuk 2:4 so as to have Habakkuk prophesy: "[Jesus], the righteous one, will live on the basis of faith"? If so, Paul uses the words of the prophet to proclaim that the faithful life of Christ reveals the righteousness of God. Or does the apostle refashion Habbakkuk 2:4 into a declaration about how believers obtain everlasting salvation on the basis of faith: "by faith, the righteous will receive life"?[7]

> The process causes us to ask important questions about these passages that perhaps we have not previously considered.

By investigating the citations in these familiar verses, the passages become even more profound. Moreover, the process causes us to ask important questions about these passages that perhaps we have not previously considered.

Allegories

The edge of allegory serves as the next vantage point that can help us see more in Scripture. Modern literature tends to limit allegory to a story where fictional characters and actions correspond to real characters and actions, such as what we see in works by Bunyan and Orwell. But in ancient literature, allegories are more generally defined. They can be as simple as a metaphor that has matured so as to expand beyond a sentence. Or, on the other end of the spectrum, they can take up an entire *pericope* and include personifications (the attribution of human traits to an impersonal concept, virtue or vice). Furthermore, there are also times where an author gives an Old Testament event an allegorical interpretation (cf. Galatians 4:22-31).

---

[7] It is even more complicated than this. For a more detailed treatment on this, see my blog post, "Punch line, Proof Texts and Paul" at http://www.hearthevoice.com/blog/74 .

Scripture is replete with allegories because the biblical authors considered the use of them important to communicate divine truth. [8] In order to understand God's Word more fully, then, we need to study biblical allegories more deeply. Such an investigation includes examining biblical allegories in their own right as well as comparing them to similar allegories that occur elsewhere in Scripture. Here are a couple of examples.

Romans 5.12-21; 6:16-19

Paul uses allegory in Romans 5:12-21 where he personifies Sin and Death in mortal combat with Grace. The allegory depicts Sin and Death as an evil queen and king who invaded God's world only to be triumphed by God's Grace. Through the act of Christ, Grace rises up to surpass Sin, dethrone Death, and restore the righteousness of God.

Therefore, just as sin entered the world through one man, and death through sin, and in this way death came to all people, because all sinned…death reigned from the time of Adam to the time of Moses…For if, by the trespass of the one man, death reigned through that one man, how much more will those who receive God's abundant provision of grace and of the gift of righteousness reign in life through the one man, Jesus Christ! … But where sin increased, grace increased all the more, so that, just as sin reigned in death, so also grace might reign through righteousness to bring eternal life through Jesus Christ our Lord.

In 6:16-19, Paul goes on to personify Righteousness as a slave owner. He argues that since we live under the reign of Grace rather than the captivity of Sin, we must offer our members as servants to Righteousness.

Don't you know that when you offer yourselves to someone as obedient slaves, you are slaves of the one you obey—whether you are slaves to sin, which leads to death, or to obedience, which leads to righteousness? But thanks be to God that, though you used to be slaves to sin, you have come to obey from your heart the pattern of teaching that has now claimed your allegiance. You have been set free from sin and have

---

[8] Allegories are part of the very nature of human thought.

become slaves to righteousness. I am using an example from everyday life because of your human limitations. Just as you used to offer yourselves as slaves to impurity and to ever-increasing wickedness, so now offer yourselves as slaves to righteousness leading to holiness.

Among other implications, by making virtues and vices come to life so to speak, these allegories enable Paul to stress the pre-eminence of grace and righteousness in his gospel while highlighting the utter folly of living in terminal sin. We gain even more insights when we compare Paul's allegory here with a similar one in James.

James 1:13-15

James also uses allegory to accentuate the roles of Sin and Death. When tempted, no one should say, "God is tempting me." For God cannot be tempted by evil, nor does he tempt anyone; but each of you is tempted when you are dragged away by your own evil desire and enticed. Then, after desire has conceived, it gives birth to sin; and sin, when it is full-grown, gives birth to death. (1.13-15, NIV)

Whereas Paul uses the allegory in Romans 5 to set up Grace's defeat of Death and Sin, James personifies Sin and Death to defend God's justice. To explain the main thrust of temptation, James presents a sexual allegory. Desire conceives and gives birth to Sin: Sin conceives and gives birth to Death. Rather than as a spurious queen and fraudulent king, here, Sin is an illicit lover with Death as her illegitimate son. Furthermore, in Romans 6, Paul uses allegory to implore us to refuse to offer our bodies as slaves to Sin. James does so to warn us of what happens when we offer her our seed.

> Examining the use of allegory in passages brings to life certain aspects and points the original authors wanted to accentuate—those which we may have a tendency to miss.

As the examples above demonstrate, examining the use of allegory in passages brings to life certain aspects and points the original authors wanted to accentuate—those which we may have a tendency to miss. Their allegories come into focus even more when we compare them to similar usages elsewhere. Now that we have discovered new insights from the vantage points of citations and allegory, let's try one last location—the rim of typology.

Typologies

As mentioned in the introduction, typologies occur when individuals or events in some manner foreshadow future people and events by describing parallel circumstances and the meanings that develop within them. Whereas a type looks forward, an antitype looks backwards. So, whereas the priesthood of Melchizedek—as the type—foreshadows the priesthood of Jesus: as the antitype, the priesthood of Jesus echoes that of Melchizedek. The antitype is often greater than the type. But it does not have to be.

All typologies are not created equal. Some are more conspicuous than others. For instance, while Paul will not let us miss that Christ is the Second Adam, his presentation in Rom 16:20 of Satan as the serpent from Genesis 3 is more enigmatic and less sustained. (Although perhaps it was more novel to the original audiences than it is to us.) Furthermore, while some typologies simply feature similarities, others begin with the similarities in order to underscore significant differences. Here are a couple of examples.

Adam and Noah

In the beginning, as described in Genesis 1-3, God split the waters, put the creatures in the world and made Adam from the dirt (Hebrew _adamah_). The man was naked in the garden and felt no shame. But then he took fruit from the tree. As a result, there was a curse, which was followed by God's gracious act of clothing Adam. From the perspective of typology we notice the connections between Adam's fall and Noah's stumble. We begin to discover hints that the Pentateuch hides in plain sight. For instance, in Noah's story, God also caused the waters over the earth's surface to recede so that the birds, the animals, and all the creatures that move along the ground could multiply on the land (8:13-18).

Further, to continue to underscore continuity with Adam, Genesis 9:20 notes that Noah was a man of the *adamah*.

It continues. As Adam took fruit from the tree, Noah took fruit from the vine. Consequently, Adam realizes he is naked, while Noah gets drunk and naked. Similarly, Noah's drunken stupor sets up a dreadful curse and the compassionate covering of his naked shame. Upon closer inspection, then, we discover that Noah is an antitype of Adam; thereby, he highlights the pitiful nature of humanity on the one hand and sets up the hope for the ultimate Second Adam on the other (see Romans 5:12-21).

Babel and Pentecost

Genesis 11 recounts how God descended to Babel and confused their tongues, so that the people could not understand each other. Then, the Lord scattered them all over the earth. He did this because: "If as one people speaking the same language they have begun to do this, then nothing they plan to do will be impossible for them (Genesis 11.6)." Similarly, in Acts 2, God's Spirit descends upon the church and causes them to speak in tongues. In contrast to Babel, the confusion comes upon the people in Jerusalem because, in the midst of all the tongues, they heard their own language being spoken.

Now there were staying in Jerusalem God-fearing Jews from every nation under heaven. When they heard this sound, a crowd came together in bewilderment, because each one heard their own language being spoken. (2:5-6)

Acts will go on to recount how the new believers are scattered throughout the world as witnesses for Christ. Moreover, while God foiled the plans of the wicked to build their tower in Babel, the typology establishes from the beginning of Acts that nothing will stop God's people from building his church.

It has been said that stopping to study the seeds results in a fuller appreciation of the flower. So also, as with citations and allegories, looking at a passage in light of typology causes us to admire and understand it all the more.

Conclusion

These examples of citations, allegories and typologies have provided only a glimpse of the type of insights you will find in the pursuing chapters. There is so much more. We are confident that the Lord will use this book not only to refresh your love for the Bible but also for him.

> It has been said that stopping to study the seeds results in a fuller appreciation of the flower.

When my family and I lived in Germany, we strolled to the city center each week to purchase the fresh, luscious produce on offer at the *Bauernmarkt* (farmers' market). When we moved back to the States, however, we had to settle for the supermarket. When we first gave my toddler a store-bought apple, he complained: "There's something wrong with this 'fwuit': it's lost its 'fwuitness.'" Our hope is that the Bible will never lose its 'fruitness' in your life and ministry—that it will never grow bland or turn stale. We write this book because we are convinced that an investigation of citations, allegories and typologies will help you experience the potency of Scripture again for the first time. Join us, as we taste and see that his Word is good.

PART ONE:

READING THE BIG STORIES MORE DEEPLY

Reading Scripture Deeply

CHAPTER 3
REDEEMING GOD'S PEOPLE

Ralph K. Hawkins

When the ancient authors of Scripture wrote their individual books, establishing intertextual links was a key part of the process. Even though each writer had something new to say, they wanted to ground their creative work in biblical traditions that had already been established.[9] They did this for at least two reasons. First, they wanted to connect what they were writing with what had gone before. What they were writing was not a new and free-standing story, but it was part of a larger story that was already in progress. Second, by linking their own writing with foregoing traditions, later biblical writers sought to establish their own textual authority for adding to the story. As Hess outlines in the Introduction, and as Dodson explains in Chapter 1, biblical writers accomplished these goals through the use of quotations, allegory, and typology.

In this chapter, we will look at how the authors of Scripture used quotations in telling the story of God's redemption of His people, and we will discuss how later biblical authors used allegory and typology to appropriate this story. The story of God's redemption of His people in the Old Testament begins with Abraham, continues through the Pentateuch, and ends with Israel's return from its exile in Babylon.[10] I will focus on the book of Joshua as a test case for looking at how its author use quotations, to appropriate former traditions to move the story forward. Joshua is an ideal book for such an experiment, because of its location in the canon. It

---

[9] See Michael Fishbane, "Types of Intertextuality." Pp. 39-44 in *Congress Volume: Oslo 1998*. Edited by André Lemaire and Magne Sæbø (VTSup 80. Leiden: Brill, 2000).

[10] In the Christian canon, the Old Testament ends with a sense that the redemption of God's people is unfinished. The final words of the Old Testament are those of Yahweh, who promises to send the prophet Elijah as a precursor to the arrival of the Messiah (Malachi 4:5-6).

comes after the Pentateuch and provides at least a partial fulfillment of the promise God made to Abraham to give his descendants a land (Genesis 12:1-7 and 15:6-15). At the same time, the book of Joshua lies at the beginning of the Historical Books, and looks ahead to a time when Israel will be at rest from its enemies, living in faithful covenant relationship with God, and serving as a light to the nations. And just as the author of the book of Joshua reaches back to appropriate the traditions of the Pentateuch, so later authors of Scriptural books reach back and appropriate the traditions contained in the book of Joshua in order to continue moving the story of God's redemption of his people forward.

Joshua Appropriates Scripture

As the first book in the Former Prophets, the book of Joshua conforms to several distinct characteristics shared by all of these books. Among other things, these books evaluate the past on the basis of God's covenant with Israel and encourage readers to devote themselves to the Lord in order to experience the covenant blessings outlined in Deuteronomy 27-28.[11] Accordingly, the Book of Joshua frequently refers back to the Pentateuch. This is sometimes done through quotations, but these quotations are often partial, sometimes consisting of just a few words. More often than not, the quotations are not word-for-word, but they are more like "echoes" in the way that passages and themes from the Pentateuch resound through them.[12] A brief survey of some of the allusions to passages and themes in the Pentateuch demonstrates the fact that the author of Joshua saw his own book as grounded in Mosaic principles.

---

[11] For a fuller discussion of the literary characteristics of these books, see Paul R. House, *1, 2 Kings*, New American Commentary 8 (Nashville: Broadman, 1995), 54-58.

[12] Richard B. Hays, *Echoes of Scripture in the Letters of Paul* (New Haven, CT: Yale University Press, 1993), 1-33.

One of the primary passages to which the author of Joshua constantly returns is Genesis 12:1-3 and 7, where God made a fourfold promise to Abraham.

The book of Joshua either directly quotes from these Abrahamic promises or alludes to them throughout.

The first aspect of the promise is that God would make Abraham and his descendants into a "nation." God worked out these promises throughout the Pentateuch, first by calling Abraham, granting

> The fourfold promise to Abraham
> (1) God would make Abraham into a great nation;
> (2) give his descendants a land in which that nation could flourish;
> (3) bless him personally, and bless those who blessed him and curse those who cursed him; and
> (4) bless all the families on earth

him an heir, and then blessing that heir with twelve sons, through whom the twelve tribes of Israel grew. The twelve tribes, however, were a loose network of interrelated peoples and not a nation. In fact, when the tribes departed from Egypt in the exodus, we are told that a "mixed crowd" (Exodus 12:38) of other ethnic groups went with them. The totality of peoples who left Egypt in the exodus, therefore, was a diverse ethnic group and not a nation. When this mass of peoples gathered around Mt. Sinai and entered into a covenant relationship with God, however, they literally *became* a nation. The Sinai covenant formed a new society of people committed to Yahweh and one another. The "mixed crowd" became "all Israel" (18:25).

After having subsequently wandered in the wilderness for forty years, these people came up out of the desert and camped on the Plains of Moab, where Moses gave them a final charge and called them to renew their commitment to the covenant. Once they had done so, he looked out upon them and said, "This day you have become a nation" (Deuteronomy 27:9). The book of Joshua begins with the Lord summoning "all this people," the "nation," to cross the Jordan River and enter the Promised Land (Josh 1, 3). Throughout the entire book, the author will refer to the Hebrew people as "all Israel" to emphasize a unified nation in contrast to the loose confederation of tribes and ethnic groups that they had been before entering into the covenant at Mt. Sinai.[13]

The second aspect of the Abrahamic promises was that God would give Abraham and his descendants a land. The patriarchs themselves were semi-nomads who wandered in the region between the Euphrates and Egypt, with a focus on Shechem, Hebron, Beersheba, and the Negev. However, if they were going to grow into a nation, this would require that they have a territory in which they could grow and flourish. The land that they would receive was "the whole land of Canaan" (Gen 17:8), and the promise of it becomes a prominent theme in the book of Genesis, repeated to Abraham and his descendants periodically throughout the book. God forewarned Israel, however, that his descendants would have to wait four hundred years before they could inherit the land, since the sin of its native inhabitants had not yet peaked (Genesis 15:13-16).

During the intervening time, Abraham's descendants suffered oppression in Egypt. God called Moses to deliver them. Following the establishment of the covenant at Mt. Sinai, God reaffirmed the promise that Israel would enter the land of Canaan (Exodus 23:20-33). As God revealed the laws by which Israel was to be governed, the text constantly repeats that these laws were to distinguish the Israelites from the indigenous inhabitants of Canaan and mold them into a distinct people in that land.[14]

The delivery of the land into the hands of the Israelites is a key focus of the book of Joshua.[15] At the very beginning of the book, the Lord spoke to Joshua, saying:

Moses my servant is dead. Now then, you and all these people, get ready to cross the Jordan River into the land I am about to give them – to the Israelites. I will give you every place where you set your foot, as I promised Moses. Your territory will extend from the desert to the Lebanon, and from the great river, the Euphrates – all the Hittite country

---

[13] E.g., Joshua 3:7, 17; 4:14; 7:23-24; 24:1.
[14] E.g., Leviticus 14:34; 18:3, 24-30; 19:9-10, 23-25, 33-34; 20; *et al.*
[15] R. S. Hess, "The Book of Joshua as a Land Grant," *Biblica* 83 (2002): 493-506.

– to the Great Sea on the west. No one will be able to stand up against you all the days of your life. As I was with Moses, so I will be with you; I will never leave you nor forsake you (Joshua 1:2-5).

The wording of vv. 3-5 is virtually the same as that found in Deuteronomy 11:24-25a. Here at the outset of the book of Joshua, a strong tie is established between Joshua and the Pentateuch, especially the book of Deuteronomy. Abraham had been promised the land of Canaan; Moses had led the people to its brink; and now Joshua would fulfill those promises.[16] Throughout the book of Joshua, the idea is present that Israel's reception of the land is a fulfillment of the Lord's promise to give it to them (e.g., Joshua 2:8; 11:23; 12; 13-21; 23:1-11; 24).

The third aspect of the Abrahamic Promises was that God would bless him personally, and that he would bless those who blessed him and curse those who cursed him. To bless someone essentially means to declare a person endowed by God with power for success, prosperity, or fertility.[17] The patriarchs had received such blessings (e.g., Genesis 14; 20; 41:37-57; 47:1-12). When the Israelites entered the land of Canaan after the exodus and wilderness wandering, some welcomed them and affirmed that they had been blessed and chosen by God, while others cursed them and opposed them. The Canaanite prostitute, Rahab, for example, makes a profound statement of faith (Joshua 2:8-11), and she in turn is blessed by being spared and assimilated into the nation of Israel (6:25).

Israel's success at Jericho and Ai, and the fact that the Gibeonites had made peace with the Israelites and were living among them, had a "domino effect." When King Adoni-zedek of Jerusalem heard about these things, he sent a message to the kings of Hebron, Jarmuth, Lachish, and Eglon, asking them to form a coalition against Gibeon (Joshua 10:1-5). Joshua defeated the Amorite coalition, which led to a campaign in which cities and regions throughout the southern districts of Canaan were

---

[16] The territory that Joshua conquered was not as vast as that outlined in Deuteronomy 1:6-8 and 11:24. The complete fulfillment of this promise did not occur until the reigns of David and Solomon (cf. 1 Kings 4:21, 24).

[17] William L. Holladay, *A Concise Hebrew and Aramaic Lexicon of the Old Testament* (Grand Rapids, MI; Eerdmans, 1988), 49-50.

conquered (10:16-43). Word of Israel's conquest of southern Canaan spread north and, when King Jabin of Hazor heard about it, he formed a coalition with the kings of the northern hill country (11:1-3). The Israelites first conquered Hazor, followed by "all the towns of those kings" (11:6-15). The second aspect of the Abrahamic promises was at least partially fulfilled in the conquest of Canaan.

The fourth part of the Abrahamic promises, that God would "bless all the families of the earth" through Abraham and his descendants, also began to be fulfilled during Israel's emergence in the land of Canaan. Israel was intended to be a blessing to all humankind, probably by reintroducing the knowledge of God into a lost and fallen world.[18] God did not create ancient Israel so that they alone could be in a relationship with him. Earliest Israel's religion was not intended to be an "ethnic religion." Instead, it was covenantal. And the central requirement of the faith was not ethnicity, but obedience to the covenant. Earliest Israel consisted of a variety of ethnic groups, all bound together in covenant (e.g., Exodus 12:38; Numbers 12:1). And when the Israelites entered the land of Canaan by way of the miraculous parting of the Jordan River, the whole purpose of the miracle was "so that all the peoples of the earth might know" about the true God (Joshua 4:24). The stories of Rahab and the Gibeonites that follow illustrate this theme that, through Israel, all humankind can come into a saving knowledge of God.[19] God gave Israel the land of Canaan in order that they might live there as his people, worship him alone, grow up as his people, and be a witness to the nations (Isaiah 40-55). Ultimately, a Messiah would rise up from among the

---

[18] The Bible does not explain how humankind would be blessed through Abraham's descendants. The call of Abraham, however, is God's response to the fall of humankind and the spread of sin throughout the world (Genesis 1-11). Clearly, God's purpose in calling Abraham and building his descendants into a nation was to reintroduce knowledge of Himself into the world.

[19] For a fuller discussion of early Israelite ethnicity and the concept of universalism, see Ralph K. Hawkins, *How Israel Became a People* (Nashville: Abingdon Press, 2013), 68-70, 137-57.

Israelite people, fulfilling God's promise that, through them, all humankind would be blessed.[20]

Another major theme in the book of Joshua, through quotations and allusions, is that of the "book of the law" of Moses (e.g., Joshua 1:13; 4:10; 8:30-35; 9:24). This is clearly a reference to the book of Deuteronomy, which presents itself as "the book of the law" (31:26). Deuteronomy could be described as ancient Israel's constitutional document. The author of the book of Joshua emphasizes Israel's obedience to that law during the period of the conquest. Throughout the book, there are numerous examples of strict obedience to the law of Moses:

- Yahweh assures Joshua that no one will be able to withstand Israel (Joshua 1:5), just as he had promised in Deuteronomy 9:2;
- the punishment of Achan is carried out in accordance with Deuteronomy 13;
- while the Israelites fall for the Gibeonites' ruse (Joshua 9), they subsequently define their relationship to them in accordance with Deuteronomy 20:10-11;
- once they had hung the bodies of the five slain kings on trees (Joshua 10:26), they were careful to remove them by nightfall (10:27), in accordance with Deuteronomy 21:23;
- the Anakim are driven out of the land of Canaan (Joshua 11:21), in accordance with Deuteronomy 9:2; and
- the Hornet is said to have expelled the enemy (Joshua 24:12), just as Yahweh had said it would in Deuteronomy 7:20.

"When the Lord had given rest to Israel from all their enemies all around, and Joshua was old and well advanced in years" (Joshua 23:1), he called the people of Israel together and reminded them of the blessings and curses of the covenant (23:14-16), just as Moses had done before his own death (Deuteronomy 28). The book of Joshua as a whole is concerned

---

[20] Herbert Bateman IV, Gordon Johnston, and Darrell Bock, *Jesus the Messiah: Tracing the Promises, Expectations, and Coming of Israel's King* (Downers Grove, IL: Kregel, 2012).

to portray early Israel in its formative years as conducting its life in a way that is subject to "the book of the law" (Joshua 1:8-9).

Joshua is Appropriated by Scripture

Throughout the remainder of the OT, biblical writers appropriate Joshua and its conquest traditions. Most of the time, later writers do not quote specific passages from Joshua about the conquest, but simply allude to the conquest events.

> Psalm 80 links the two events: You brought a vine out of Egypt; you drove out the nations and planted it. (Psalm 80:8).

There are several examples of this in the Psalter, such as Psalm 78, a famous hymn in praise of God's historical guidance of Israel. In this passage, the writer simply alludes to the conquest, explaining that "He drove out the nations before them and allotted their lands to them as an inheritance; he settled the tribes of Israel in their homes" (78:55). Even though Psalm 78 only alludes to the conquest, these words, "drove out," "allotted," and "inheritance," provide direct linguistic connections to the commands in Deuteronomy to carry out the conquest traditions in the book of Joshua.

Rather than directly quoting from or alluding to the conquest traditions specifically, biblical authors usually allude to the exodus and conquest as if they were a single event.

The later prophets allude to the conquest traditions in the same way, using one or two words to establish linguistic connections either with the instructions about the conquest in the Pentateuch or in the account of the conquest in Joshua. For example, in one of the oracles of judgment against Israel, God rehearses the saving actions he performed in bringing Israel out of Egypt and into the Promised Land:

I destroyed the Amorite before them,
though he was tall as the cedars
and strong as the oaks.
I destroyed his fruit above
and his roots below.
I brought you up out of Egypt,
and I led you forty years in the desert
to give you the land of the Amorites.
(Amos 2:9-10).

When the text says that God "destroyed" the Amorites to "give" the Israelites their land, it is using terms right out of the pages of the Pentateuch and the book of Joshua. God had promised Moses and the Israelites that He would destroy the Canaanites (e.g., Deuteronomy 7:17-26) so that the Israelites could possess their land (e.g., Numbers 33:52, 53, 55), and Joshua records at least the partial fulfillment of those promises using the same terminology. Not only did God empower the Israelites to "destroy" the Canaanite population (e.g., Joshua 6:21), but He fought on Israel's behalf himself, destroying more of them than the Israelites were able to kill by themselves (10:11).

Likewise, the New Testament frequently appeals to the conquest traditions in order to connect God's ongoing redemptive activity with Israel's past.

Paul uses the language of "inheritance" here, portraying Israel's possession of the land as the fulfillment of the patriarchal promises (e.g., Genesis 13:14-18; 15:18-21). The book of Hebrews traces the theme of "rest" from the Old Testament through the New Testament. The author of the book notes that God, in his anger, swore that following the exodus, the rebellious generation would not enter God's rest because of their unbelief (Hebrews 3:11, 16-19). The author's readers may have assumed that Joshua gave the Hebrews their rest when he led them into Canaan, but he explains that this was not the case,

> **The book of Acts linking back to Joshua**
>
> In his speech to the Sanhedrin, Stephen saw the conquest as providing the vital transition from the patriarchal period to the time of Israel's establishment as a nation in its own land (Acts 7:44-47). When the apostle Paul preached in the synagogue in Antioch, he explained that, after God had chosen Israel's ancestors and made the people great during the Egyptian sojourn, he led them out of Egypt, through the wilderness, and into Canaan. "After he had destroyed seven nations in the land of Canaan," Paul explains that "he gave them their land as an inheritance (Acts 13:17-19).

For if Joshua had given them rest, God would not speak later about another day. So then, a Sabbath rest still remains for the people of God; for those who enter God's rest also cease from their labors as God did from his. Let us therefore make every effort to enter that rest, so that no one may fall through such disobedience as theirs (Hebrews 4:8-11).

While Paul describes Jesus as the second Adam, Hebrews enjoys yet another connection. The "rest" to which Joshua was leading his generation was the Promised Land. Unfortunately, his leadership did not bring the people into the rest they so longed for, and true "rest" still lies in the future. Only Jesus, the New Testament "Joshua," makes true divine rest possible (Hebrews 4:14-16). The author of Hebrews urges faithful Christians to strive toward it (4:1, 11) by being faithful to their confession of faith in Christ (4:14) and persevering in obedience to him as Lord (4:2, 6, 11).

In 1 Peter, the apostle wrote to encourage persecuted believers in Asia Minor to stand firm for Christ. After greeting his readers, Peter reminds them that Jesus' resurrection has secured a "living hope" and "an inheritance that can never perish, spoil or fade – kept in heaven for you" (1 Peter 1:3-4). While Peter does not quote the book of Joshua, his use of the word "inheritance" alludes to the Abrahamic promises and to the conquest traditions, which had never been entirely fulfilled. Peter explains that Jesus would bring a permanent inheritance. In the next chapter, Peter quotes about half of Exodus 19:6 to make the point that all Christians, including Gentile Christians, share in God's covenant with Israel:

But you are a chosen people, a royal priesthood, a holy nation, a people belonging to God, that you may declare the praises of him who called you out of darkness into his wonderful light (1 Peter 2:9).

Peter alludes to the conquest traditions by the use of one word – an allusion that is unclear in the NIV. When Peter says that his readers are a people "belonging to God," he literally says that they are his "possession," a word that hearkens back to the Pentateuch and to Joshua. At the beginning of the Mosaic covenant, God took Israel as his own "possession" (Exodus 34:9). God would plant the Hebrews in the

Promised Land, which was theirs to "possess" (Deuteronomy 7:1), but it was imperative that they understand that they themselves were to be God's own "possession" (Deuteronomy 7:6). Building on the exodus, wilderness, and conquest traditions, Peter makes the point that believers of all races are finally unified in Christ (1 Peter 2:9-10).

The last passage we will mention here is the Great Commission (Matthew 28:18-20). In this passage, Jesus' disciples gather in Galilee, where they encounter the risen Jesus. Since "some doubted (v. 17), Jesus reassured them that "all authority in heaven and on earth has been given to me" (v. 18), and he charged them to "go and make disciples of all nations, baptizing them in the name of the Father and of the Son and of the Holy Spirit, and teaching them to obey everything I have commanded you. And surely I am with you always, to the very end of the age" (vv. 19-20).

This passage echoes Joshua 1 in several ways. Just as Jesus assured his disciples that he had been given authority, so God assured Joshua that he would have Mosaic authority (e.g., Joshua 1:3, 5, 9). Just as Jesus charged the disciples with the task of teaching converts to be obedient to God's commands, so God charged Joshua with leading the people in the careful observance of God's instructions (e.g., 1:7-8). And just as Jesus assures the disciples of his abiding presence, so had God assured Joshua that he would be with him always (1:5, 9). Just as God's presence had empowered Joshua for his mission at this important juncture of Hebrew history, so the New Testament Joshua empowers his people for mission in the new age.

Conclusion

In this chapter, we saw how the book of Joshua uses intertextuality to tell the story of how God redeemed his people. Joshua appealed to earlier traditions through heavy use of

> There were no human heroes in the conquest. Instead, God was the sole actor.

quotations and echoes in order to move the story of God's redemption of his people forward. Likewise, later authors appropriated the book of Joshua through the use of direct quotations, echoes, and typology in order to continue to move the story of God redeeming his people forward. We can make several significant observations about how the biblical writers perceived those traditions. First, the literal interpretation of the conquest is never challenged or corrected throughout the entire Bible. Second, biblical references to the conquest do not usually contain references to specific battles or human personages, but understand the conquest as God's action.

Third, the conquest was a watershed event in the progress of redemption that led to the initial fulfillment of the Abrahamic promises and covenantal blessings. However, this fulfillment was only partial and did not bring about the completion of redemption. For later biblical writers who appropriated these traditions, the conquest served as a type for the great day when God would finally and climactically establish his kingdom.

CHAPTER 4
HOW TO PRAY AND LIVE WISELY

Michael D. Matlock

A part of the centrality of Christian theology is the notion that the triune God offers mercy and forgiveness to all sinners. But, even many Christians who believe this central tenet of the faith often do not believe that God will extend mercy and forgiveness to sinners that are deemed worse than other sinners. Can the God whom Christians call Lord forgive and have mercy on an adulterer, a racist, a rapist, a molester, or a murderer? How about someone who has committed these sins repeatedly? How about for someone who has caused another person to commit some wrongdoing, or a group of people, or even a nation? What if a person committed heinous evil acts against millions of people? If we are honest with ourselves, almost everyone has viewed sin on an indefensible sliding scale. So, can the worst of sinners or offenders receive mercy and forgiveness from God?

> We should find out the purpose of the intertextuality. Some possible purposes include indicating fulfillment, discontinuity, obedience or disobedience, theological development, reminding, and many other possibilities. Some of these options are discussed in other chapters in this book.

This issue of the Christian life requires in-depth biblical, theological, psychological and philosophical answers. The aim of this chapter is to explore part of the conversation between biblical texts and one key Second Temple Jewish (or intertestamental) text in the area of penitential prayer to discover how they converse with each other and what they might communicate through quotation and allusion. Both are primary means of employing inner-biblical exegesis or intertextuality.

There are a couple of key things to keep in mind when trying to understand how scriptural texts build upon other scriptural texts or, stated more crassly, how the "the Bible is full of itself."[21] First, one's study of Scripture needs to observe how Scripture and Second Temple Jewish texts "handle" or "put to use" Scripture. We need to determine, if possible, which points are emphasized and which principles are used.

Second, Christians committed to understanding and living according to the truths of God's word must become more familiar with the biblical books and the Jewish literature of the Second Temple so as to be able to notice the literary and theological import into Old and New Testaments passages. Second Temple texts contain an invaluable supplementation for our understanding of the canonical Scriptures. Too many expositors of the word of God view the period between the Old and New Testament (hereafter OT and NT) as "four hundred years of [divine] silence." Neither Yahweh nor his people were silent during this phase of salvation history.

> When there are long parallel accounts in Scripture as with the two great narratives of Israel's history, there will be many quotations and allusions. Not surprisingly, in the versions of Manasseh, king of Judah and Hezekiah's son, the Chronicler reproduces the portrayal of 2 Kings 21 very closely in biographical details.

Again, several chapters in this book take up this point so stay alert to see how these books help us to read God's word deeply.

Parallel Scriptural Testimony in 2 Kings 21:1-18 and 2 Chronicles 33:1-20

We all recognize that the four Gospels tell the same story of Jesus from different perspectives. Likewise 1-2 Kings and 1-2 Chronicles retell many of the same stories. While the four Gospels record the relatively same brief history of the life, death, and resurrection of Jesus Christ, by comparison, Samuel-Kings and Chronicles span a much larger period of

---

21. James Sanders, *Biblical Intercontextuality: The Bible is Full of Itself*, DVD, 50 min. (Washington, D.C.: Biblical Archaeology Society, 1999).

time. [22] The primary reasons to create a new parallel account of events or sayings is both to communicate again the common features among the parallel accounts, and also to point out subtle and not so subtle ways of viewing the same event or saying from a different angle. Knowing and revering the books of Samuel and Kings, the writer of Chronicles interprets Israel's prior history differently because the people of his era face new challenges to their life and faith.

Kings and Chronicles attribute to Manasseh a laundry list of heinous actions: rebuilding high places, erecting altars to Baal and making an Asherah pole(s), bowing down to the starry hosts and worshipping them, sacrificing his children in a fire, practicing divination, seeking omens, and consulting mediums and spiritists. Beyond these transgressions, many other points of comparisons are noted in the two accounts.

But the Chronicler adds some surprising information about Manasseh. Whereas the historian in 2 Kings 21:11-18 (cf. Jeremiah 15:4) continues to relate many more of Manasseh's detestable actions and the Lord's judgment, in 2 Chronicles 33:11-20, we are told that Manasseh was captured by the king of Assyria and taken prisoner to Babylon where something amazing happens. In this foreign prison, Manasseh prays a penitential prayer and the Lord responds and brings Manasseh back to Judah (vv. 12-13). Manasseh leads a wonderful physical and spiritual restoration, and in vv. 18-19 the author alerts us that the events of Manasseh's reign, particularly his penitential prayer, were written in the "annals of the kings of Israel" and the "records of the seers." This is an important detail that several early Jewish interpreters will take up in their writings.

---

22. See Ralph Klein's comparative charts of these two histories at http://fontes.lstc.edu/~rklein/

The Prayer of Manasseh: A Second Temple Jewish Text[23]

Written sometime between 200 B.C. and A.D. 50., the Prayer of Manasseh is a Jewish prayer of repentance attributed to King Manasseh.[24] Although it is not a canonical text for Protestants or Roman Catholics (however, it appears in an appendix to the NT in the Latin Vulgate Bible), nevertheless this penitential prayer became an important liturgical text in the Eastern Orthodox churches. The prayer also functions as a canticle for morning prayer in the *Book of Common Prayer* in the Anglican traditions of the Church. Luther and the translators of the King James Version of the Bible *included* this prayer in the other important books for understanding Scripture section known as the Apocrypha to Protestants.

It is written from the first person singular perspective, "I," and clearly is a penitential type of prayer, as moving from ascription to confession to petition. As a prayer of repentance, the pray-er seeks to persuade the Lord to take some action in the future, here the immediate future. It is easy to conclude that the Bible teaches that obedience leads to blessing and disobedience leads to curse. However, one discovers a dissimilar message contained in this prayer largely taken from the context of Chronicles and other sources. Setting the scene in a Babylonian prison, the Chronicler recounts a very different, more remorseful Manasseh than the one communicated by the historian in 2 Kings 21:1-18 as noted above. This later Second Temple Jewish book, the Prayer of Manasseh (Pr Man), creates for the reader what the author imagined was the content of Manasseh's prayer as indicated in 2 Chronicles 33:12-13.[25] The Prayer of

---

[23]. View http://www.biblegateway.com/passage/?search=Prayer%20of%20Manasseh%201&version= CEB for the CEB translation.

[24]. For lengthy penitential prayers in the OT which the Prayer of Manasseh emulates, see 1 Kings 8:22-53; 1; Ezra 9:5-15; Nehemiah 1:4-11; 9:4-37; Daniel 9:3-19; and Psalm 51.

25. The extrabiblical lore surrounding Manasseh is also evident in another Early Jewish community, the Qumran community. See 4Q 381 (Non-Canonical Psalm B) in Géza Vermès, *The Complete Dead Sea Scrolls in English* (New York: Penguin, 1997). The superscription reads "Manasseh, king of Judah, when the king of Assyria imprisoned him."

Manasseh is structured in this manner: A) Invocation (vv. 1-8); B) Confession of Sin (vv. 9-10); C) Petition (vv. 11-15):

A prayer of Manasseh[26]

1.1 O Lord Almighty, God of our ancestors, of Abraham and Isaac and Jacob and of their righteous offspring; 2 you who made heaven and earth with all their order; 3 who confined the sea by your word of command, who shut the deep and sealed it with your fearful and glorious name; 4 before whose powerful presence all things quiver and shake 5 for the majesty of your glory is unendurable, and the wrath of your threat to sinners is irresistible 6 yet immeasurable and unfathomable is your promised mercy, 7a for you are the Lord Most High, tender-hearted, long-suffering, and abounding in mercy, and you repent over the evils of humankind. 7b O Lord, according to your great goodness you have promised repentance and forgiveness to those who have sinned against you, and in the multitude of your mercies you have appointed repentance for sinners, for salvation. 8 Therefore you, O Lord, God of the righteous, have not instituted repentance for the righteous, for Abraham and Isaac and Jacob, who did not sin against you, but you have instituted repentance for me, who am a sinner.

9 For I have committed sins more numerous than the sand of the sea; my transgressions are multiplied, O Lord, they are multiplied! I am not worthy to gaze and see the height of heaven because of the multitude of my iniquities. 10 I am bent over with many an iron chain so that I am rejected because of my sins, and there is no remission for me because I have provoked your wrath and have done evil in your presence setting up abominations and multiplying idols.[27]

---

[26] Author's translation.

27. "Idols" is the same word used in the High Priest Simon's prayer (3 Maccabees 2:18) to describe the would-be words of Ptolemy IV Philopator and his forces who desire to desecrate the Jerusalem temple by entering the Holy Place. From Simon's vantage point, if Ptolemy was allowed to enter and trample the Lord's temple, Ptolemy would say he was able to do

11 And now I bend the knee of my heart, imploring you for your kindness. 12 I have sinned, O Lord, I have sinned, and I acknowledge my transgressions. 13 I earnestly beg you, forgive me, O Lord, forgive me! Do not destroy me with my transgressions! Do not be angry (with me) forever nor store up evil for me; do not condemn me to the depths of the earth. For you, O Lord, are the God of those who repent, 14 and through me you will manifest your goodness; for, although I am unworthy, you will save me according to your great mercy,

15 and I will praise you forever and for all the days of my life. For all the host of heaven sings praise to you, and yours is the glory forever. Amen.

Drawing from the Greek translation of 2 Chronicles 33, the author of the Pr Man recontextualizes and recreates numerous allusions— a word, a brief phrase, or an image that constitutes an indirect reference but can be traced to a source. Some of the more notable allusions are as follows:

Pr Man 10 "I provoked your wrath" alludes to 2 Chronicles 33:6 "[Manasseh did much evil before] the Lord to provoke him [the Lord] to anger (translations are mine for each of these allusions)."

Pr Man 10 "[I was] multiplying idols" alludes to 2 Chronicles 33:7 "he set the graven image, the molten image, the idol which he made, in the house of God."

Pr Man 10 "I am bent over with many an iron chain" alludes to 2 Chronicles 33:11 "[they took] Manasseh in bonds, and bound him in fetters, and brought him [to Babylon]."

Pr Man 11 "And now I bend the knee of my heart, imploring you for your kindness" and Pr Man 1 "the God of our ancestors" allude to 2 Chronicles 33:12 "he was greatly humbled before the face of the God of his fathers."

Going beyond the notion of echo, the implied author recalls these phrases and images of Manasseh with their context in order to dramatize

---

just what he did with the pagan temples containing idols, thereby setting the Lord's sacred place on par with the pagan temples.

further the situation for the reader who is familiar with Chronicles. It is in the context of 2 Chronicles 33 that Manasseh humbles himself, repents of his sins, and prays; as a result, the Lord returns Manasseh to the land. Clearly, this prayer is an intertextual expansion of 2 Chronicles 33.

Moreover, the numerous echoes from the life of David indicate the author's desire to connect in some measure this Prayer of Manasseh text with the thankful nd penitential David found in various portions of Scripture such as 2 Samuel 7:18-29; 1 Chronicles 16:8-36; 17:16-27; and Psalm 51. There is much intertextuality with Psalm 51 in the confession and petition sections of the Prayer of Manasseh. Psalm 51 is arguably the quintessential prayer of the penitent sinner in all of the Bible. It is also written from the first person singular perspective.

Along with David's prayer after being promised a perpetual dynasty (2 Samuel 7:25, 27; 1 Chronicles 17:24), only a select few prayer texts in the OT and Second Temple literature contain Manasseh's beginning vocative, "O Lord Almighty:" (1) the angel in Zechariah's first vision (Zechariah 1:12), (2) Jeremiah (Jeremiah 15:16), and (3) Baruch (Baruch 3:1, 4). Manasseh's second vocative, "God of our ancestors, of Abraham and Isaac and Jacob," echoes another phrase, "LORD, the God of our fathers Abraham, Isaac and Israel," from one of David's prayers of praise (1 Chronicles 29:18). Another

> There are quotations and allusions to numerous ideas in Psalm 51 such as God's abundant mercy (Psalm 51:1 = Pr Man 7a), the pray-er's transgressions and knowing the pray-er's transgressions (Psalm 51:3 = Pr Man 9), doing evil in the sight of God (Psalm 51:4 = Pr Man 10), justification in God's punishment (Psalm 51:4 = Pr Man 5), petition for God not to remember sins Psalm 51:1,9 = Pr Man 13), request not to be banished nor destroyed (Psalm 51:11 = Pr Man 13), and a promise to praise God because of deliverance (Psalm 51:14-15 = Pr Man 14-15).

point of contact with David stems from the many parallelisms and the common motif between the Prayer of Manasseh and 1 Chronicles 21 in which David disobeys the Lord by taking a census of the people. He receives the Lord's punishment along with his mercy.

Yet, precisely and specifically through Manasseh's emphasis on the patriarchs in vv. 1 and 8, the author of the prayer creates an unusual picture of God not recognizable from the corporate penitential prayers in the OT. The patriarchs, "Abraham and Isaac and Jacob," and their offspring are "righteous," but Manasseh describes himself as the opposite, a "sinner" and not one of the righteous patriarchal offspring. This is a radical change from the OT prayer of repentance; yet, Manasseh makes an even more stunning remark: God instituted "repentance" for sinners like Manasseh, not for righteous people such as the patriarchs and their offspring. In v. 7b, Manasseh indicates that along with repentance God also promises "forgiveness" for sinners to ensure their salvation. This divine promise of forgiveness, not for the righteous but for sinners, is the most explicit reference of its kind in all of the Second Temple Jewish literature.

Another major theological departure from other penitential prayers is found in the divine attribute formula—"The LORD, the LORD, the compassionate and gracious God, slow to anger, abounding in love and faithfulness, maintaining love to thousands, and forgiving wickedness, rebellion and sin" (Exodus 34:6-7a). In another lengthy penitential prayer in the OT, the Levites (Nehemiah 9:17) took this divine attribute formula and adapted it to the context of the disobedient actions of the Israelites in refusing to enter the promised land.[28] In the Prayer of Manasseh, there are two noteworthy modifications to the formula.

First, rather than use the more common Greek word for "merciful," the author of the Prayer of Manasseh uses "tender-hearted." The second change is more significant in that God is described as "one who repents over the evils of humankind" just as the same modification appears in Jonah 4:2 and Joel 2:13. The phrase is ambiguous as it may indicate two different meanings: (1) being sorrowful over the sins

---

28. Another point of intertexture with the Levites' prayer is in the description of God as the one who 'made the heaven and the earth" (cf. Pr Man 2; Nehemiah 9:6).

committed by people, or (2) relenting from God's punishment in the face of humanity's suffering. Given the connections to 1 and 2 Chronicles and more specifically the parallelisms with 1 Chronicles 21, the second meaning is more probable in Manasseh's prayer.

In vv. 7b-8, the Prayer of Manasseh indicates that the relenting in which the Lord engages (v. 7a) demands a similar relenting/repenting from humans in regards to their sinfulness. This "repentance" is provided and demanded by the Lord. The fractured divine-human covenant relationship may continue as common ground for both parties through God's provision of repentance.

In vv. 11-14, Manasseh's petitions for forgiveness contain some of the most eloquent phrases of penitential prayers in all of the Second Temple Jewish literature. First, Manasseh describes his penitential action as "I am bending the knee of [my] heart" in v. 11. As mentioned, God relents and demands a similar response from humans, and this is exactly the type of response in which Manasseh is engaging himself. His actions of idolatry and rebellion have been exchanged for humility and contrition. Second, Manasseh's confession of "I have sinned, O Lord, I have sinned" in v. 12 is beautifully balanced by his supplication "Forgive me, O Lord, forgive me" in v. 13. By the end of v. 13, Manasseh makes a remarkable counterpoint to his previous comment about God as "God of the righteous" in v. 8. Manasseh now sees himself in God's fold because God is "the God of those who repent" (v.13).

Manasseh's prayer represents an opposing perspective over and against the dominant discourse of other interpreters of Bible history which prevailed in the postexilic period. This penitential prayer is part of a growing treatment of divine punishment and forgiveness in late Second Temple Judaism.[29] This prayer is a motivation for repentance and a renewed hope for a mended relationship with the Lord for even the worst of offenders. The employment of the divine attribute formula with modifications affirms the abundant compassion of the Lord and the length

29. See also Philo, *On Rewards and Punishments* 163-64; Pseudo-Philo 12, 15, 19, and 21; and *Testament of Gad* 5.

to which the Lord reaches to restore his sinful, rebellious people. The Prayer of Manasseh shares much in common with Psalm 51 and offers many new considerations for repentance and its valued practice for a person of God.

Penitential Prayer in a Parable in Luke 18:9-14

When we search for penitential prayers in the NT, we notice them strangely absent. Nevertheless, we can see the impact of penitential prayers found in the OT and Second Temple Jewish texts. Let us consider a parable told by Jesus in Luke's Gospel that may have been influenced by the Prayer of Manasseh and other penitential prayers found in the OT like Psalm 51. In Luke 18, Jesus makes two larger points about praying in two parables. In the first parable (Luke 18:1-8; cf. 11:5-8), the so–called "parable of the unjust judge," Jesus teaches his disciples to pray persistently when praying for something that God desires. If an unjust judge who does not honor the laws of God can be influenced to act by nonstop appeals of a widow, how much more will our just God act to uphold his people when they beg him? In this first parable, Luke addresses a narrow topic of prayer, namely persistence. In the second parable, Luke opens the discussion of prayer more widely and announces the necessity of repentance.

> If we think back on the life of Manasseh, particularly if we gloss over his prayer, do we presume, as did this Pharisee, that we are so much more righteous than Manasseh was and all the other "bad people out there?" Are we so foolish to reckon that we do not need God's mercy because we are not "bad people" like this tax collector or Manasseh?

In the second parable (Luke 18:9-14), Jesus highlights two types of prayers from two very different people, a Pharisee and tax collector. Luke tells his readers that this parable is intended for "some who were confident of their own righteousness and looked down on everyone else." The Pharisee is confident in his prayer; he is pious, living an honest and upright life. Although the law required a person of God to fast only once a year on the Day of Atonement, this Pharisee exceeds requirements by fasting twice a week. He tithes on all of his income, not just the required parts. At the heart of his prayer, there is a contrast to all the bad sinners in the world, of which he proudly does not belong.

In stark contrast to the Pharisee's prayer, Jesus relates two telling differences in the tax collector's prayer. First, he does not stand up in a prominent place to pray, but rather stands far away from the Temple to pray with his eyes and hands lowered. Second, the tax collector pounds out (literally) a confession of his sinful condition and appeals for God's mercy. His words are, "God, have mercy on me, a sinner." Because of his contrite, humble attitude and prayer, he stands justified before God. Remember, the tax collector is viewed by the people who have access to God's word as the scum of the earth. Yet, this is not the case in reality. Everyone is a sinner, and there is not a sliding scale for each person's sin. The qualitative difference in all people is not their sin, but rather their genuine penitential prayers.

Conclusion

From these inner-biblical or intertextual connections made in texts recounting Israel's history, in penitential prayers, and in a parable about such prayer, we can learn some important points about the Christian faith and life. Comparing our lives to other "bad" people is a dangerous game to play. We may just end up trading the central thing that brought us into a right relationship with the triune God, namely knowing and believing that our righteousness is only possible through the righteousness of our Lord and Savior, Jesus Christ. Second, we may forget that the most liberating thing we can do is confess our sins, both ones of omission and commission, and bask in the forgiveness of our gracious and merciful God. God is no respecter of persons; we are all loved the same no matter what sins we have committed. Third, we learn and benefit from penitential prayers such as Psalm 51 and the Prayer of Manasseh. When we confess our sins and receive God's forgiveness, we are not only justified before God as Jesus' parable teaches us. But, we are also liberated to praise God with our whole beings. After all, praising God is what we were created to do.

Chapter 5
Hearing God's Prophets

Beth M. Stovell

The Old Testament prophets have much to share with their readers. However, sometimes our expectations about what we will find when we read the Old Testament prophets can cause difficulties in the process of interpretation. These difficulties often center around two key issues: fulfillment and allegory. This chapter will first examine these two issues. It will then demonstrate the importance of hearing God's prophets by analyzing Isaiah 5 itself. This will in turn show how knowing Isaiah 5 helps us to interpret how John 15 is using Isaiah 5 to highlight Jesus' identity and our identity in relationship to him.

There are at least two ways in which issues of fulfillment impact Christians. First, at times Christians see the fulfillment of the Old Testament in the New Testament as a replacement of Israel with the Church. Other Christians believe we know what the Old Testament prophet is saying only in light of the New Testament. This can sometimes mean that we read the Old Testament as though the New Testament already existed; but at the time that the Old Testament authors were writing, they were wrestling with their situations as they sought to follow Yahweh at their time in history prior to the creation of the New Testament. It is important for us to begin with the prophets' own stories in order to understand how these stories then fit in with the larger story of the Bible. This is where the issue of fulfillment comes in. In order to understand fulfillment, we must first understand that the prophets were not primarily fore-telling some future event that would occur hundreds of years later, but were primarily sharing a vision for the people within their community in their own time. This vision for their people continued to have significance when we reach the New Testament. The New Testament authors, seeing this significance, particularly in the person of Jesus, saw the

Old Testament prophets as giving the first picture of something that would be filled out to its fullest at a later time. This connects to the Jewish concept of "greater than this." Jews believed that if God did something meaningful in the past, He would not only do it again, but would do something that was greater than the first event. As primarily a group of Jews, Jesus' disciples saw him as the "greater" version of what God had already done in the past with the Israelites. Thus, when Jesus "fulfills" the Old Testament prophecies, he fills them full of even greater meaning. This does not negate the original meaning of the Old Testament Scriptures, but gives them greater depth and understanding.

Besides understanding fulfillment, it is necessary to understand the concept of allegory in order to interpret many sections of Old Testament prophecy (see the Introduction for a definition of allegory). It is also helpful to understand how an allegorical method is used to read a piece of literature. This approach to allegory is about finding the spiritual meaning that is hidden in the text.[30] At times, this can happen when the New Testament authors read the Old Testament. Both of these aspects will be important as we discuss how John 15 uses Isaiah 5.

The Old Testament prophets used metaphors frequently and, in some cases, extended these metaphors as allegories across entire chapters (and even books) of Scripture. In the case of Isaiah 5, in order to understand Israel's complicated relationship with Yahweh, the prophet Isaiah describes Israel as Yahweh's vine in Yahweh's vineyard.

As a way of exploring the value of Old Testament prophets both to the New Testament authors and to us today and of exploring the significance of allegory for understanding the Old and New Testaments, this chapter will first examine the allegory of Israel as a vine in Isaiah 5 and will then examine how this allegory is used in John 15.

Isaiah 5

The metaphorical description of Israel as vine and vineyard occurs in several of the prophets' writings as well as the Psalms. Examples in the Old Testament of the metaphor of Israel as vine metaphor include Psalm

---

[30] See Gordon Teskey, "Allegory." Pp. 43-60 in *The Spenser Encyclopedia*. Edited by A. C. Hamilton..(Toronto: University of Toronto Press, 1990).

80:8-16; Isaiah 5:1-7; Jeremiah 2:21; Ezekiel 15:1-8; 17:5-10; 19:10-14; and Hosea 10:1. Of these depictions of Israel as a vine, Isaiah 5's description is one of the earliest and the most extensive. Many of the other Old Testament descriptions appear to build on Isaiah's allegory. In order to understand what Isaiah's allegory is intended to mean, it is helpful to get a sense of the context in which Isaiah 5 occurs in the larger story of the book of Isaiah.

In Isaiah 5, God is putting together an indictment against Israel. The book of Isaiah is structured like a court case. God is setting up a case against Israel for violating their covenant with him. Israel has aligned themselves with other nations instead of depending on God. Specifically, what was once a united kingdom under King David has now split in two with a northern kingdom calling itself "Israel" and a

> Vines and vineyards are common imagery in the ancient world because they would have been part of the common experiences of the people of Israel. Unlike our modern world where vineyards are a place to visit, vineyards were an essential part of Israel's economy.

southern kingdom calling itself "Judah." The northern kingdom aligned itself with Assyria, trying to gain from Assyria's wealth and military power. However, rather than do positive things in return for the northern kingdom, Assyria conquered the northern kingdom. The book of Isaiah begins with an awareness of these events.

Isaiah 5 acts as the prelude for Isa 6 where Isaiah the prophet is called to speak to God's people. Isaiah 5 provides a poetic description of the difficult situation that is facing God's relationship to Israel. Isaiah 5's allegory includes two major elements: God is a gardener and Israel/Judah is a vine/vineyard. Isaiah 5:1 sets up the allegory as a "song" that the prophet is singing for the one he loves. Rather than stating outright that the "loved one" is God at the start of the "song," Isaiah leaves this piece of information until v. 7 when he explains that "The vineyard of the Lord Almighty is the house of Israel and the people of Judah are the vines he delighted in." This delay allows the hearer to hear the song and its description of God's care for the vineyard before knowing the passage speaks about them.

Isaiah 5:2 focuses on all of the hard labor the gardener put into tending his vineyard (for example, he "planted it with the choicest vines,") and on his expectation of a good crop. It ends by stating that, to the gardener's disapointment, this vineyard "yielded only bad fruit." In Isaiah 5:3–4, God asks the people of Judah to act as judge between him and his vineyard. God puts forward his case: he did everything he could to take care of this vineyard. Due to the vineyard's inability to produce good fruit, in Isaiah 5:5–6, God describes what he will do to his vineyard. He will allow the vineyard to be destroyed by leaving it unprotected (v. 5) and allow it to become a wilderness, uncultivated and unwatered (v. 6).

Isaiah 5:7 shifts from the "song" to an explanation of what the "song" means. This verse explains that this song is an allegory. Isaiah explains that God is the gardener and the vineyard is the house of Israel, the people of Judah are the vines. As is common in Hebrew poetry, this

> Similar to Isaiah 5, several Minor Prophets condemn God's people for calling evil good and good evil. Micah 3:1 condemns to leaders of Israel as those who "hate the good and love the evil." Amos 5:7 speaks of the Israelites as "you that turn justice to wormwood, and bring righteousness to the ground!" Amos 5:15 encourages them to return to the correct ordering of good and evil: "Hate evil and love good."

phrase may be developing a parallel to create emphasis. The second half of Isaiah 5:7 explains what finding "only bad fruit" means in reference to Israel. Isaiah explains that God "looked for justice, but saw bloodshed; for righteousness, but heard cries of distress." In other words, God looked for people to be treating each other and God well, and instead they mistreated each other and neglected God.

To understand the meaning and significance of this allegory in Isaiah 5:1-7, it is helpful to see how it would have been read in Isaiah's time. A hint to this understanding comes in the "woes" that follow Isaiah 5:1–7. What Isaiah 5:1–7 explains in terms of metaphor Isaiah 5:8-30 explains in terms of the situation of the people's actions toward one another and toward God. These verses describe the concrete ways that Israel rejected God as the source of provision and instead stored up wealth for themselves. In the quest for their own gain, the people begin to "call evil good and good evil…and put darkness for light and light for darkness" by mistreating their fellow Israelites through bribery and unfairness in the court systems. Instead of honoring God, they seek their own entertainment, believing their own cleverness. God states that he will judge this arrogance and injustice with his justice that promotes humility. He will take Israel's leaders out of their positions of power.

John 15

With Isaiah 5 and its allegory of Israel as a vine and God as a vine gardener in mind, we now will examine how an awareness of this section of Old Testament prophecy provides helpful grounding for a familiar New Testament passage. In this section, we will examine Jesus' statement in John 15: "I AM the True Vine".[31] In order to understand this passage, we must first understand where John 15 fits in relation to the story of John's Gospel.

John 15 sits near the end of John's Gospel and it sits in the middle of what is commonly called "The Farewell Discourses" in John 13-17. Throughout John 13-17, one of the key themes is remaining. This was an important message as the disciples were about to face the loss of their leader. Up to this point in the story, the Jewish leaders have first become angry with Jesus and then, in John 12, these leaders began plotting Jesus' death. In the Farewell Discourses of John's Gospel, Jesus is aware that his death is impending and for this reason he shares his final messages with his disciples and prays to God for the disciples and for the world. Jesus also shares aspects of his identity with the disciples and tries to explain to them his role in the world. In John 13, Jesus predicts that he will be betrayed by one of the disciples and he predicts Peter's betrayal. In John

---

[31] To learn more about the metaphors in John's Gospel, see Craig Koester, *Symbolism in the Fourth Gospel: Meaning, Mystery, and Community* (Minneapolis: Fortress, 2003).

14, Jesus explains that while there will be suffering and difficulty for the disciples after his death, he will leave the Spirit with them to comfort them.

John 15 picks up on these themes of the upcoming death of Jesus by describing a key aspect of Jesus' identity: Jesus as the true vine. John 15:1 describes Jesus as the true vine and the Father as the gardener. John 15:2-3 describes two kinds of branches: the ones who bear fruit and those who do not. John 15:4 emphasizes the need to remain in Jesus, the vine, in order to be among those who bear fruit. John 15:5-8 demonstrates the impact of remaining in Jesus: the Father's judgment for those who do not remain in Jesus and the Father's glory and naming as "disciples" for those who do remain in Jesus.

We can read this allegory without knowing its Old Testament background and still yield some fruitful and godly wisdom. However, when we read John 15 with a knowledge of its use of the Old Testament prophets, it opens up new and fuller ways of understanding the text that would have been part of what John was thinking about when he wrote his gospel.

Isaiah 5 appears to be the source for the first part of the passage in John 15. As explained above, in Isaiah 5 the two main characters are God as gardener and Israel as the Vine. In John 15, these main characters are repeated and given some additions. God is still gardener (in the form of the Father), but instead of Israel, Jesus is the Vine. Awareness of Isaiah 5 allows us to see John's point more clearly, that Jesus is the fulfillment of Israel as the vine; Jesus represents the true

> Throughout John's Gospel, the Evangelist describes Jesus as pointing to the true Israel in a variety of ways. Jesus is the Good Shepherd correcting the bad shepherding of Israel's leaders similar to the depiction of God as Shepherd in Ezekiel 34. Jesus is described as "the Word" and "the way," terms often used of the Law. Jesus is the embodiment of the true place of God's presence as temple imagery is frequently used of Jesus throughout the Fourth Gospel.

Israel who followed God. In John 15, the allegory in Isaiah 5 is extended. The vine is not what produces fruit in and of itself. Instead, the details of the vine are made clear in John 15 through the addition of the language of branches. Jesus as the vine is a good vine, but all of the branches who might be connected to Jesus as vine take advantage of this goodness. As in Isaiah 5, not all parts of the branches are responding properly to God's provision. In Isaiah 5, this rejection is met with judgment as in John 15: the branches that do not bear fruit will be cut off. Notably, the rejection of God's provision found in Isaiah 5 is specifically linked to Jesus as the source of this provision in John 15. Judgment of the branches that reject Jesus will be "like a branch that is thrown away and withers; such branches are picked up, thrown into the fire and burned" (v. 6). This judgment echoes the second half of Isaiah 5 in its description of judgment against those of Israel who have rejected their God. An awareness of Isaiah 5 helps to characterize reasons for this judgment in John 15: the Israelite leaders have believed in their own wisdom, seeing what is evil as though it were good. This is consistent with the experience of persecution that both Jesus and his followers will experience (John 15:18-25).

An understanding of Isaiah 5 makes us aware that when Jesus says he is the True Vine, he is doing more than describing himself as a source of sustenance. He is also identifying himself with the people of Israel. Unlike the vine in Isaiah 5, which did not bear good fruit because of its disobedience, Jesus as the *true* vine acts as *true* Israel would, obeying God in all ways. Describing himself as the vine, Jesus is also describing himself as the means by which the branches are able to yield good fruit or not. By dividing the vine from the branches in the metaphor and by Jesus' description of himself as the vine, Jesus has made himself the pathway to pleasing God.

Conclusion

There are several ways that starting with the message in the prophets helps us to better value the Old Testament prophets themselves as well as have a richer picture of the New Testament message.

As we have seen in this chapter, examining Isaiah 5 highlights important themes that continue to be relevant in today's world. These themes exist in themselves without having to move to the New Testament account in order to gain them. For example, Isaiah 5 reminds us of the need to be aware of forms of idolatry that exist today. In Isaiah 5, God's critique of Israel surrounds how they value wealth and partying, but are unaware that God made everything that allows for their wealth. They "call evil good and good evil". Today, the world around us lacks an awareness of God's creation and provision. At times, in a desire for wealth and status, Christians today can be led to call things that are actually evil good, while denouncing the good as evil. When we place our wealth or our need for security above our treatment of one another and above God, this can be one form of idolatry we experience today. Isaiah 5 reminds us that this looks like bad fruit.

Besides concern for idolatry in our midst and the need to return to the Lord, analysis of Isa 5 in relation to John 15 refocuses analysis of the modern reader on Jesus' Jewish roots. At times, we read Jesus in light of modern European traditions where Jesus is blond, blue-eyed, and looks like your average "white guy". But Jesus' heritage was Middle Eastern. His culture and religious background was Judaism. John's use of the metaphor of the vine places Jesus in a long history of Jewish hope and expectations. Jesus fulfills these promises of the Jews, but this does not mean that the Church has now replaced Judaism, but rather that Christians stand in continuity with the hope established within the Hebrew Scriptures and within early Jewish culture itself.

Reading Isaiah 5 and examining John 15 in its historical context also provides a greater nuance to what it means to "remain" in Jesus in John 15. The concept of "remaining" cannot and should not be associated primarily with whether someone stays in a Christian congregation or not. Isaiah 5 suggests that remaining is more about the content of a person's actions, mind, and heart than their location in the community. In fact, the Israelites remained in community with one another, but did not live like they cared for one another or like they knew God. In the context of John's Gospel, one of the important factors of remaining is maintaining hope in God's faithfulness despite Jesus' death and the suffering that will accompany this. We too live in a situation where evil is still present in our midst and we experience the suffering that comes along with that evil. As with the disciples, we are called by Jesus to remain true to God in the face of this suffering and evil. While great suffering exists, so does great hope in the experience of the Spirit (as John 14 describes) and in the knowledge of Jesus' ultimate return. We remain faithful as we live attached to Jesus Christ our true vine.

Reading Scripture Deeply

CHAPTER 6

THE GOOD NEWS OF JESUS
TYPOLOGY IN THE GOSPELS AND
ACTS

Joseph R. Dodson

After reading the Gospels for the first time, one of my students announced in class: "You know, Jesus reminds me a lot of Harry Potter." I started to chuckle, but then I remembered as a kid being ridiculed for saying that Jesus reminded me of E.T. [32] When I revealed this childhood scar to them, the students were emboldened to divulge the characters that reminded them of Jesus. They mentioned the likes of Superman, Gandalf, Forest Gump, and Doctor Who.

> "Failing to notice these typologies might cause us to miss crucial truths about the Messiah that God intended for us to catch."

I told my students that I was not sure if J.K. Rowling and Steven Spielberg intended for the boy wizard and the extra-terrestrial to remind us of Jesus. But the Gospels do use typology so that Jesus will remind us of certain Old Testament figures. It is as if the Evangelists wanted us to say: you know, Jesus reminds me a lot of Isaac, of Joseph, of David, and so on. As we walked through some of these typologies, my students began to notice that each one accentuates various characteristics of Christ and his

---

[32] In my defense, I explained my adolescent reasoning: E.T. descended from another world. While on earth, he died, came back to life, and then ascended back into the heavens. For more on Jesus and E.T., see http://markgoodacre.org/podcasts/NTPod57.mp3

mission.[33] They also started to recognize that—in contrast to the Hollywood imitations—failing to notice these typologies might cause us to miss crucial truths about the Messiah that God intended for us to catch.

As mentioned in chapter 1, typologies occur when individuals or events in some manner foreshadow future people and events by describing parallel circumstances and the meaning that develop within them. Sometimes the Evangelists used typology to say that Jesus was "like" an Old Testament figure. At other times the authors did so to say that Jesus was "greater than" one of these characters. And as we will see below, sometimes it is to say that Jesus "is" a certain figure. Often what begins as faint echoes to an Old Testament figure turns into loud notes as a narrative progresses.

In this chapter, we will provide examples of how (1) Matthew presented Jesus as the prophet like Moses, (2) how Mark depicted him as a miracle worker like Elisha, and (3) how John presents the Lord as Lady Wisdom. Further, we will consider how (4) Luke goes the other direction and presents Stephen as a martyr like Jesus. (5) Finally, we will use Matthew's presentation of Mary to demonstrate how the evangelists can use typology with respect to other characters besides Christ. These examples are meant to be representative rather than exhaustive. Moreover, they are intended to be introductions rather than in-depth studies.

Jesus reminds me of Moses

In Deuteronomy 18, Moses proclaims:"The Lord your God will raise up for you a prophet like me from among you, from your own people. You must listen to him…"

The Lord said to me: "What they say is good. I will raise up for them a prophet like you from among their people, and I will put my words in his mouth. He will tell them everything I command him. I myself will call to account anyone who does not listen to my words that the prophet speaks in my name (vv. 15, 17-19).

Because of this passage, by the time we get to the New Testament, the Jews expected this prophet like Moses in addition to a Davidic King. Matthew demonstrates that Jesus is both; but he uses typology to reveal the former.

Of the Four Gospels, only Matthew includes the story of the infanticide committed by Herod during Jesus' childhood. From the angle of typology, the king's plot to slaughter the Hebrew babies evokes the crime of Pharaoh and the similar situation surrounding Moses' birth. It is as if from the start Matthew wants us to think, "You know, Jesus reminds me a lot of Moses." And the hints keep coming. To flee Herod's wrath, Joseph takes Jesus to Egypt—the place Moses was born and raised. Matthew even highlights the event by quoting Hosea 11:1, a verse that originally referred to the Exodus: "Out of Egypt I called my son."

> It is as if from the start Matthew wants us to think, "You know, Jesus reminds me a lot of Moses." And the hints keep coming.

The parallels don't stop there. As Moses spent forty years in the wilderness, Jesus stays there for forty days. While in the desert, Satan tempts Jesus three times. And three times Jesus responds by citing scripture: all of which originated from the mouth of Moses (Deuteronomy 8:3; 6:16; 6:13). One of the highpoints of Moses' life was when he went onto a mountain to receive God's Law. Interestingly enough, of all the Evangelists, only Matthew records Jesus' Sermon on the Mount. In Matthew 5-7, Jesus goes upon a mountain and reinterprets Moses' Law. Jesus insists, however, that he did not come to abolish the Law of Moses. He came to fulfill it. "Not the smallest letter, not the least stroke of a pen, will by any means disappear from the Law until everything is accomplished" (5:18).

In light of Deuteronomy 18, then, the audience's astonishment at the end of Jesus' sermon should not come as a surprise to us. They were "amazed at his teaching, because he taught as one who had authority, and not as their teachers of the law" (7:28). The typology underlines the reason.

Unlike the teachers of the Law, Jesus is the prophet like Moses. He speaks the very words of God. He proclaims all that God has commanded him. The typology also sounds a warning from Deuteronomy 18:19: God will call to account everyone who fails to listen to the words of *his* Prophet.[34]

Jesus reminds me of Elisha

Whereas the First Gospel depicts Jesus as the new Moses to emphasize the authority of his teaching, Mark presents Jesus as greater than Elisha to underscore the Lord's power. Of all the prophets in Israel, Elisha has arguably the most impressive resume for healings and miracles—that is, until we get to Jesus. With this in mind, when we read the story of Jesus cleansing the leper in Mark 1, we should be reminded of Elisha, the only other prophet attributed with healing a man from leprosy.

In 2 Kings, Naaman went to Elisha's house for help. The prophet commanded him: "Go, wash yourself seven times in the Jordan, and your flesh will be restored and you will be cleansed" (2 Kings 5:10). It took some convincing, but the army commander eventually swallowed his pride and went down to the river to take his dips. As soon as he was finished, "His flesh was restored

> Whereas the First Gospel depicts Jesus as the new Moses to emphasize the authority of his teaching, Mark presents Jesus as greater than Elisha to underscore the Lord's power.

and became clean like that of a young boy" (5:14). Similarly, in Mark 1, a leper approached Jesus for help. In response, Jesus reached out his hand, touched the man and said: "Be clean!" Immediately the leprosy left him and he was cleansed (1:41-42). As you can see, both Elisha and Jesus cure the incurable disease, and in each case the leprosy quickly disappeared. But in contrast to Naaman who has to wash himself seven times in the Jordan, Mark's leper is healed by a single touch from Jesus.

---

[34] Cf. Acts 2:22-23

Furthermore, the story of Jesus bringing the young girl back to life in Mark 5 should remind us of the similar story when Elisha resuscitates a young boy. In 2 Kings 4, a mother accosts Elisha so that he goes to her house to save her son. Upon arrival, he went into the room and found the boy dead on the couch. He shut the door on the two of them and began to pray. ·

He got on the bed and lay on the boy, mouth to mouth, eyes to eyes, hands to hands. As he stretched himself out on him, the boy's body grew warm. Elisha turned away and walked back and forth in the room and then got on the bed and stretched out on him once more. The boy sneezed seven times and opened his eyes. (2 Kings 4:33–35)

Similarly, in Mark 5, a synagogue leader approached Jesus and begged him to come to his house and heal his daughter. When Jesus arrived, he took the child's father and mother as well as his disciples into the room to see the child. There, Jesus grabbed the girl by the hand and said "Rise up, little girl!" She immediately stood up and began to walk around. While Elisha had to give the boy mouth to mouth—eye to eye and hand to hand—resuscitation, Jesus simply took the girl by the hand. Elisha's healing of the boy was prolonged, but Jesus cured the girl instantly. For instance, whereas the prophet had to walk around the room before the boy was revived, the girl rose from her bed without hesitation and began to walk around.

Perhaps the most remarkable parallel between Elisha and Jesus occurs in 2 Kings 4:42-44 and Mark 6;37-42. In the former, Elisha commanded his servant to feed the crowd with the only bit of bread he possessed—twenty loaves. The servant demurred: "How can I set this before a hundred men?" But Elisha insisted, "Give it to the people to eat. For this is what the Lord says: 'They will eat and have some left over.'" So the servant set the bread before them. And, as God promised: "they ate and had some left over, according to the word of the Lord" (v. 44).

Likewise, in Mark 6, Jesus commanded his disciples to give the crowd something to eat (v. 37). But like Elisha's servant, the disciples pointed out the apparent flaw in the master's plan: there's only five loaves of bread. Jesus takes the food anyway, gives thanks for it and hands it to the disciples to distribute. "They all ate and were satisfied" (v. 42). Unlike 2 Kings, however, Mark saves some of the final numbers for the end of the story to increase the dramatic effect. Whereas Elisha fed a hundred men with twenty loaves: with only five loaves, Jesus fed *five thousand*. While Elisha had some leftovers, Jesus had *twelve baskets full* of them. Therefore, the point of the typology becomes clear. Jesus is not simply a miracle worker like Elisha: he is a miracle worker greater than Elisha.

Jesus reminds me of Lady Wisdom

In Proverbs, Wisdom makes the extraordinary claim to have been with God at creation. She proclaims:

> I was there when he set the heavens in place,
>
> when he marked out the horizon on the face of the deep,
>
> when he established the clouds above
>
> and fixed securely the fountains of the deep,
>
> when he gave the sea its boundary
>
> so the waters would not overstep his command,
>
> and when he marked out the foundations of the earth.
>
> Then I was constantly at his side.
>
> I was filled with delight day after day,
>
> rejoicing always in his presence,
>
> rejoicing in his whole world
>
> and delighting in humankind. (Proverbs 8:27-31)

We learn even more about Wisdom and her role in Genesis from a book in the Greek Old Testament called the *Wisdom of Solomon* (a popular work for Christians during the time of John). As other Jewish works around this time, the *Wisdom of Solomon* refers to God's "Wisdom" and his "Word" interchangeably.[35] For instance, in the parallelism of 9:1, it says

---

[35] Do not let Logos as Lady Wisdom throw you. That Logos was a masculine term while Wisdom was a feminine figure did not pose a problem for most writers. As far as I know, only Philo struggled with this.

God "made all things by his Word; by his Wisdom, he formed humankind."

What is more, the *Wisdom of Solomon* draws from Genesis and Proverbs 8 to present Wisdom and the Word less as an attribute of God and more as a personal being who shares in the Lord's divinity. According to the author, Wisdom is the breath of God's power, the pure emanation of his glory, the reflection of his eternal light. She is a spotless mirror of his work, the very image of his goodness (*Wisdom of Solomon* 7.25-26). Shining brighter than the Sun, Wisdom outshines all the stars, because she is greater than the light. Therefore, "she is not succeeded by the night," that is to say, "against her evil does not prevail" (7:29-30). According to the author, God sends Wisdom from his throne. She descends from heaven to proclaim what is pleasing to the Lord (9:10), to bring people near to God and to grant them everlasting life (6.18-19).

In light of this understanding of Wisdom, let's read the familiar passage in John 1:1-5. Keep in mind that the terms Wisdom and Word were used synonymously in the Greek Old Testament and other Jewish Wisdom Literature. The Fourth Gospel begins with these well-known words:

In the beginning was the Word, and the Word was with God, and the Word was God. He was with God in the beginning. Through him all things were made; without him nothing was made that has been made. In him was life, and that life was the light of all people. The light shines in the darkness, and the darkness has not overcome it.

The similarities are striking. In both the Wisdom of Solomon and the Gospel of John, Wisdom and the Word were with God in the beginning; they were agents of his creation; and they provide humanity with life and light.

John uses this typology *not* to say that Jesus is like a man. Christ is not presented as being like Moses or greater than Elisha. Moreover, John

---

Nevertheless, rather than separating them as distinct figures, Philo claims—despite her name—Lady Wisdom is masculine. In short, Philo gives Lady Wisdom a beard.

does not even use the typology to say that Jesus is simply *like* Wisdom, like the Word, or even like God. Rather, the typology proclaims that Jesus *is* the Wisdom and Word of God (cf. 1 Corinthians 1:24). Thereby, John's typology establishes a high Christology from the start: as Wisdom and the Word, Jesus is the one who shares in God's divinity.

Stephen reminds me of Jesus

In the examples above, Jesus is meant to remind us of Moses, Elisha, and Lady Wisdom. But New Testament authors can also go the other direction. For instance, in Acts, Luke depicts Stephen as a Christ-like figure. The typology starts with Luke's introduction of Stephen with lofty praise that attributes to him qualities that remind us of Jesus. "Stephen, a man full of God's grace and power, performed great wonders and signs among the people" (Acts 7:8). As with Jesus, the religious leaders engaged Stephen in debate; and, as did Jesus, Stephen

> John's typology establishes a high Christology from the start: as Wisdom and the Word, Jesus is the one who shares in God's divinity.

dominated his opponents in the theological contest (v. 10). Consequently, he too was forced to give an account in court as he faced accusations from false witnesses. So similar is the setting, it is enough to cause *déjà vu* among those who know the Gospels.

In response to the charges, Stephen—with the bright face of an angel (v. 15)—launches into a sermon that incites the crowd to stone him. Here, the parallels become even more pronounced. Both Jesus and Stephen made proclamations about the Son of Man at God's right hand. During his trial, Jesus proclaimed: "From now on, the Son of Man will be seated at the right hand of the mighty God" (Luke 22:69). Similarly, during his execution, Stephen calls out: "I see heaven open and the Son of Man standing at the right hand of God" (Acts 7:56). In case we've missed it, Stephen's last words confirm the typology:

1) "Lord Jesus, receive my spirit" (Acts 7:59), and

2) "Lord, do not hold this sin against them" (7:60).

In his Gospel, Luke records two sayings of Jesus that the other Evangelists omit:

1) "Father, forgive them, for they do not know what they are doing" and

2) "Father, into your hands I commit my spirit" (23:34; 46).[36]

Following the typological suit, Stephen's prayer requests help us avoid missing the connection Luke intends for us to make. Therefore, just as typologies can delineate an aspect of Jesus' character, they can also highlight the continuity of his character with that of his followers. Thus, Luke leads us to say, "you know Stephen reminds me a lot of Jesus."

Mary Reminds Me of Some "Scandalous" Ladies

There are other typologies at work in the Gospels and Acts that center on other figures besides Jesus. [37] For instance, the genealogy in Matthew 1 sets up a fascinating typology. Matthew cuts against the grain of many Jewish genealogies by including women in his. But he does not list the likes of Sarah, Rachel, and Rebekah as one might expect. Rather, Matthew points out the more provocative ladies in the line of Judah—Tamar, Rahab, Ruth, and "Uriah's wife." Despite the diversity of these women, their stories have something in common: questionable sexual backgrounds.[38] Two of the women have a past in prostitution; one was involved in an indecent proposal and the other in an affair.

> In view of typology, these stories set up the seemingly scandalous situation of the final woman listed in the genealogy—Mary, the mother of Jesus.

With the inclusion of these women, Jesus' family tree becomes shady. Why does Matthew choose to include these women in Christ's Genealogy? If we consider this question in view of typology, we see these

---

[36] The first of these sayings may not have been in the original manuscript of Luke.

stories set up the seemingly scandalous situation of the final woman listed in the genealogy—Mary, the mother of Jesus. But all of these women share more than seemingly illicit backgrounds. Each of them—to different degrees—was finally vindicated. In the end, Judah counts Tamar as righteous. Joshua presents Rahab as a paragon of faith. Boaz, the righteous man, marries Ruth. Bathsheba gives birth to Solomon—the wise heir of Israel's throne.

And Mary is vindicated all the more. The angel of the Lord emphatically denies an illegitimate conception: "what is conceived in her is from the Holy Spirit." (When one realizes that it is God who is to be born, one is no longer surprised to find a virgin giving birth.[39]) Like Ruth, a righteous man does not reject her. Like Bathsheba, she will go on to give birth to the Son of David. In contrast to Bathsheba, however, Mary gives birth to Israel's everlasting king. As a result of Mary's faithfulness, "Now one greater than Solomon is here (Matthew 12:42)."

Application

We began this discussion by mentioning a student in class who said Jesus reminded him of Harry Potter. At the end of the class, another student approached me. He was clearly upset. In contrast to the young lady who had only recently read the Gospels, he explained that he "grew up in church." He bemoaned that even though he knew all these stories he had never seen the connections. I encouraged him to take heart because we often know facts without paying attention to them. I challenged him to go back through those old familiar stories with these typologies in mind so that what is clear to him about Jesus and the Gospels can become even clearer. As we have seen, we can read Scripture and be richly blessed without ever seeing these connections between stories, the allegories, or the typologies. Yet, when we read Scripture deeply and see these subtle treasures, we draw more benefit from our studies. As the student and I walked out of the classroom together I reminded him that the Evangelists underscored these typologies *not* so that we would only be informed about Christ but so that we would be significantly transformed by him—so much

---

[39] See Augustine, Sermon 370.3.

so that when people look at our lives they would say, "you know, they remind me a lot of Jesus."

CHAPTER 7

FALSE TEACHERS IN THE EPISTLES

Caryn A. Reeder

The letters of the New Testament often incorporate Old Testament and Second Temple traditions to explain Jesus, the early church, and the world. These connections make the story of Jesus and the early church part of the story of God's people through time. This claim has major theological significance, of course, and it also has practical importance for the early church: the church can expect God to act as God has always acted. In 2 Corinthians, 1 Timothy, 2 Peter, and the letters of Revelation, typologies drawn from earlier traditions apply this message to the problem of false teaching.

False teachers were a great danger in the very early church. The church of the first century had no seminaries to train leaders, no Adult Education classes—in fact, no Bible, yet.[40] Instead, the church had traveling apostles who established local churches and then moved on. This practice left space for misunderstandings and incorrect teachings to arise, or for false teachers to spread unorthodox messages (see, for instance, Galatians 1:6-9, 2 Thessalonians 2:1-3, or 2 John 7-11).

In this chapter, we will first explore how the writers of Revelation and 2 Peter used typology to characterize false teachers. In these books, the stories of famous deceivers like Balaam and Jezebel and notorious sinners like the pre-flood generation and the inhabitants of Sodom and Gomorrah represent the danger of and judgment on false teachers. In 2

---

[40] In the first century, owning even one book of the Bible was rather expensive. A copy of Isaiah would cost over $1000 (in today's dollars). Perhaps one of the reasons Jesus quotes from Deuteronomy, Isaiah, and Psalms is because Nazareth's synagogue could only afford one book each from the law, the prophets and the writings; see E. Randolph Richards, *Paul and First Century Letter Writing* (Downers Grove: IVP, 2004), especially pp. 165-69.

Corinthians and 1 Timothy, on the other hand, the typologies center on the audiences of false teachers. The example of gullible Eve provides warning of the dangers of deception. Through these typologies, the early church's experience becomes a repetition of history, and the church can therefore know how to respond.

Revelation

Like most apocalyptic literature, Revelation is chock-full of references to the Old Testament and Second Temple texts. The author, John, scatters key words, quotations, names, and more throughout the book. The allusions to earlier texts and traditions help explain John's visions. Of course, the use of the Old Testament in Revelation needs an entire book of its own.[41] Here, we will focus on the typology of false teachers in Revelation 2:14 and 20-23.

According to John, the false teachers at work in Pergamum and Thyatira teach that it is okay for Christians to eat food sacrificed to idols and to be sexually immoral (an issue often connected with idolatry in the Bible, both literally, as in Numbers 25:1-3, and metaphorically, as in Jeremiah 3:6-10). In other words, the message of the false teachers is that Christians can participate in idolatry without compromising their faith. This message may sound pretty strange, considering the strong condemnation of idolatry across the Bible. It was a popular teaching in the early church, though, because of the social context of the Roman world.

Temples were part of everyday life in antiquity. A person might stop by a temple to worship, or offer sacrifices of supplication or thanksgiving. But temples were also places to meet with professional colleagues and transact business. The local and imperial governments met in temples, and official documents could be stored in temples. Birthday parties and celebrations were held in temples. In this context, a pagan who converted to Christianity would not simply be changing the identity of the god she worshiped, or the place in which she worshiped. She would be

---

[41] See e.g., Dave L. Mathewson, A New Heaven and a New Earth: The Meaning and Function of the Old Testament in Revelation 21.1—22.5. Library of New Testament Studies 238 (London: T&T Clark, 2003).

cutting herself off from her business connections, government, and friends. Conversion to Christianity would disrupt her life completely. This context helps explain the message of the false teachers of Pergamum and Thyatira. These people claimed that a Christian could go to temples for business or parties without actually committing idolatry. John, however, disagrees. The typologies of the false teachers such as Balaam and Jezebel support his condemnation of their message.

In Numbers 22-24, Balaam the prophet was hired by Balak of Moab to curse the Israelites. Although the cursing did not work out as Balak intended, the Israelites did indeed get into trouble with the women of Moab, entering their beds—and the worship of their gods (Numbers 25:1-3). According to Numbers 31:16, Balaam was the mastermind behind this seduction. Because of Balaam, the Israelites ate food sacrificed to idols, became involved in sexual relationships with Moabite women, and were punished by a plague (25:8-9).

This story is the final story of Israel's failings in the wilderness before the entry into the Promised Land. It lingers in the mind, and later traditions like Joshua 22:17, Psalm 106:28-29, and Hosea

> Was Jezebel a real person or simply a symbol of the false teachers in Thyatira (like Balaam)? While we can't know for sure, it is likely that there was a woman in the church who claimed to be a prophet and taught, like the Nicolaitans, that it was okay to participate in the cultic life of the city. Her name probably was not Jezebel, though— her name is John's way of warning his readers against her message.

9:10 show the power and horror of the story in the Israelite imagination. John draws upon this horror by incorporating the story of Balaam into the letter to Pergamum. The false teachers, called the "Nicolaitans," in Pergamum are just like Balaam, teaching God's people to commit idolatry. Just as all the Israelites seduced by Balaam's plan were destroyed (Deuteronomy 4:3), so also John warns that if the church in Pergamum does not repent and turn away from the Nicolaitans' message, Jesus will make war against them with the sword coming from his mouth (Revelation

2:16; cf. 1:16). This typology of the Nicolaitans makes the danger of their teaching clearly evident, in a vivid and memorable way.

John also takes the church at Thyatira to task for allowing the prophet Jezebel to teach and "mislead" Christians to commit acts of sexual immorality and to eat food sacrificed to idols. The name of this false teacher comes from the story of the daughter of the king of Sidon who married Ahab, king of Israel. After their marriage, Ahab built a temple to Baal in Samaria and also set up sacred poles for worship (1 Kings 16:31-33). We might guess from this story that Jezebel brought the worship of her gods with her when she married Ahab, and indeed 1 Kings 21:25 attributes Ahab's actions to the urging or, even better, seduction of his wife.

In Revelation 2:20-21, the church in Thyatira harbors just such a "Jezebel" who misleads Christians into sexual immorality and idolatry. The comparison of the false teacher in Thyatira with the queen of Israel characterizes the false teacher as a corrupting influence in the heart of the community. John warns that "Jezebel" and her "children"—that is, those who follow her teachings—will suffer and die. The first Jezebel was thrown out a window and eaten by dogs following the death of her son, and her remaining children and followers were also killed (2 Kings 9:24-10:25); the second Jezebel will be tossed onto a bed of suffering, and her children killed (Revelation 2:22-23). The imagery of Revelation 2:20-23, influenced by the dramatic story of Jezebel in 1 and 2 Kings, makes apparent acceptance of "Jezebel" in Thyatira all the more appalling.

The stories of Balaam and Jezebel offer parallels to what is happening in Pergamum and Thyatira. In this way, the churches are warned against the danger of false teaching. The comparisons have deeper implications as well. Both Balaam and Jezebel were foreigners, outsiders who disrupted and endangered the people of God with their idolatrous messages. By comparing the false teachers of Pergamum and Thyatira with these famous foreigners, John is implicitly identifying the Nicolaitans and "Jezebel" as foreigners. These typologies separate the false teachers from the members of the church, giving the churches even more reason to reject the teaching.

2 Peter

The two typologies of false teachers in Revelation 2 are strong, and send a powerful message to the audience. The typologies of false teachers in 2 Peter 2 rely on more general comparisons, perhaps because of the more general nature of the accusation against them: these teachers are accused of "destructive heresies," licentious behavior, greed, and exploitation (2:1-3).[42] The connections drawn between these teachers and earlier traditions rest more on character than on the act of false teaching, or the message of the false teachers.

The introductory verses in 2 Peter 2 end with a promise of judgment on the false teachers, a promise which is supported by examples of the condemnation of the wicked in the past in vv. 4-8. The first example, angels who sinned and were punished, comes from ancient Jewish interpretations of Genesis 6:1-4. In 1 Enoch 6-10, the "sons of God" of Genesis 6 are fallen angels, who are chained up and thrown into deep pits to await the final judgment. The second example in 2 Peter 2 is drawn from the flood:

1 Enoch is a compilation of texts dating from as early as the third century BC to as late as the second century AD. It contains a series of visions about the depravity of the world and God's judgment, using the story of Genesis 6:1-8 as a model—or, we might say, a typology—of the destruction of the wicked in the last days. In the New Testament, Jude 14-15 refers to 1 Enoch, so at least some people in the early church were familiar with it.

the ungodly were destroyed, but the faithful Noah and his family were

---

[42] 2 Peter's false teachers may also be among the scoffers who teach that Jesus is not going to return (3:3-4). This message gained power in the early church when the first generation of Jesus' followers died before Jesus' return. The scoffers in 2 Peter claim that the promised return of Christ was a lie.

saved. The third example concerns the wicked cities of Sodom and Gomorrah, which burned as the righteous Lot escaped. Each example is introduced by "if," and the three "if" statements culminate in a "then" in v. 9: if these wicked people of the past were destroyed but the righteous were protected, then the wicked false teachers in the church will also be judged while the faithful are saved.

In 2 Peter 2:10-19, the false teachers are described as slanderers, irrational animals, accursed children, waterless springs, slaves of corruption, and as followers of Balaam, who was so enamored of the wages of sin that he had to be rebuked by a donkey (vv. 15-16). This particular example, and the comparison drawn from it, highlights the difference between the typologies made in Revelation and 2 Peter. While the examples of Balaam and Jezebel in Revelation focus on the *issue* of false teaching, the examples listed in 2 Peter 2 are instead concerned with the *character* of the false teachers. The comparison with the wicked characters from earlier biblical and Jewish traditions reassures the church that the false teachers in their midst will be judged, and the faithful in the church will be kept safe. The church need not fear them, nor heed their message.

The typologies of 2 Peter 2 are interesting for two reasons. First, the examples given in this chapter are largely taken over from the book of Jude. In Jude, the same examples identify corrupting influences in the church; 2 Peter adapts the examples to the more specific problem of false teachers. 2 Peter gives us a great example of the layers of interaction of biblical and Second Temple texts: the Old Testament influences Second Temple traditions like 1 Enoch, which then influence Jude, which then influences 2 Peter. The layers tie these disparate texts together, making the churches represented in Jude and 2 Peter part of the ongoing story of God's people.

The second point to notice is the presence of the faithful in the typologies. The wicked pre-flood generation is contrasted with Noah and his family; the inhabitants of Sodom and Gomorrah are contrasted with Lot. The inclusion of these righteous people who were saved from judgment and punishment extends the typology to include the faithful in the church. The false teachers will be judged, just as in the past—and the faithful will be saved, just as in the past.

2 Corinthians and 1 Timothy

The final two letters we will consider in this chapter are slightly different from Revelation and 2 Peter. Instead of focusing on the message or character of the false teachers, the typologies in 2 Corinthians and 1 Timothy are concerned with the people deceived by false teachers. Both letters use the story of Eve in Genesis 3 as a warning and lesson for the potential victims of deception.

The church in Corinth had many problems, from chaotic worship to sexual immorality to the presence of the "super apostles." Paul worries that the super apostles would teach the Corinthians a different Jesus, Spirit, or gospel than Paul himself taught (2 Corinthians 11:4). He worries that "just as Eve was deceived by the serpent's cunning, your minds may somehow be led astray from your sincere and pure devotion to Christ" (v. 3).

2 Corinthians 11:3 is not Paul's only reference to Genesis 3. In Romans 5:12-21, Paul draws an analogy between Adam and Jesus. Adam's sin brought sin, condemnation, and death to all people; Jesus' righteousness brought grace, justification, and life. Romans was written after 2 Corinthians, but Paul wrote the letter to the Romans while he was visiting the church in Corinth, and he introduces the same typology of Adam and Jesus in 1 Corinthians 15:21-22 and 45-49. The Corinthians would have been familiar with Paul's understanding of Jesus as the new (and improved!) Adam, and the church as the new creation (note 2 Corinthians 5:17).

The introduction of Eve and the serpent spins the typology in a new direction. Paul identifies the super apostles with the cunning serpent in 2 Corinthians 11:3, and in vv. 14-15, he likens the super apostles to Satan—masters of disguise who will end in judgment (see also Romans 16:17-20). Both comparisons highlight the deceitful character of the super apostles, which in turn supports the typology of the church as the new Eve. Eve was deceived by the serpent (Genesis 3:1, 13), and the church is in danger of being deceived by these false apostles. Eve is a particularly powerful representation of this danger to the church because of Paul's new creation theology. The church may be a new creation, but the danger of deception remains. The church must hold to what Paul has taught them in order to remain in the new creation.

Eve's second, and final, appearance in the New Testament comes in the instructions given to women in the church in 1 Timothy 2:11-15. Women are here commanded to learn "in quietness and full submission," but forbidden to teach or "assume authority" over men (vv. 11-12). This text, of course, sparks heated debates in the church today. It likely would have been quite controversial even in the early church! The New Testament shows that women were important leaders in the early church (e.g., Matthew 28:1-8; Luke 8:1-3; Acts 16:14-15 and 18:26; 1 Corinthians 1:11 and 11:5). Paul even names ten women in Romans 16:1-16 and Philippians 4:2-3 as his colleagues in ministry, preaching and teaching just like Paul and his male colleagues. The instructions in 1 Timothy seem not to reflect the normal practices of the early church. Eve's presence in this text helps explain its different perspective.

> The argument about "creation order" doesn't really make sense of the biblical story. In Genesis 2, man—"Adam"—is created first, then the animals, and then the woman, which would mean the woman is inferior to man and to animals. In Genesis 1, humans are created last, so therefore, by this argument, fish and birds and beasts are superior to women and men! "Creation order" is not a very good argument, as Paul himself recognizes in 1 Corinthians 11:11-12.

The women in 1 Timothy are prohibited from teaching or taking on authority over men *because* Eve was created after Adam, she was deceived, and she sinned (2:13-14). Modern discussions of this text often get stuck in v. 13. Interpreters sometimes suggest that because the woman was created second, she—and therefore all women—must be inferior to men. But perhaps there is something else going on here. Adam was the first to be created, and he alone heard the command regarding the tree of the knowledge of wisdom and evil (Genesis 2:17). As emphasized in Romans 5:12-21, Adam sinned by disobeying and eating the fruit.

However, the woman was created second, after Adam. She was not present to hear the command given by God. The story in Genesis 3 suggests that the crafty serpent tricked her into sin, as 2 Corinthians 11:3 claims—and this deception is also key in 1 Timothy 2:13-14.

The church addressed in 1 Timothy has been targeted by teachers of myths, genealogies, ascetic practices, and other false doctrines (1:3-7, 4:1-7). The women in the church, especially the "young widows," seem to be particularly susceptible to these teachings, learning to be idle, to run around, and to gossip (5:13). This depiction makes the widows sound like the stars of *Desperate Housewives of Ephesus*. Note, however, the end of v. 13: they say what they should not say (cf. Titus 1:11), and because of this, some of them have "turned away to follow Satan" (1 Timothy 5:15). In other words, these women are being deceived by the false teachers at work in the church.

According to 1 Timothy 5:14, the young widows should be encouraged to get married and raise families. The implication here is that family life will keep the women busy, with no time to waste on the false teachers. This instruction is similar to 1 Timothy 2:15: "she will be saved through childbearing, if they remain in faith and love and holiness with self-control" (my own translation). Read together with 5:14, this verse could be claiming that women will be kept safe from deception by means of bearing children and raising families.

There is an alternative interpretation of 1 Timothy 2:15. The first verb in the verse is singular ("she will be saved"), and the "she" in view is most logically Eve. In Genesis 3:15-16, Eve's punishment is pain in bearing children, but there is also a promise that her offspring will crush the serpent's head. That offspring is Jesus, and his birth from Eve's descendant Mary is the means of salvation for all women. Comparable to the typology of Adam and Jesus in Romans and 1 Corinthians, Eve's deception and sin is undone by Mary's faithfulness.

1 Timothy 2 and 5 picture danger in the church: false teachers are targeting idle widows, and these widows are then spreading the false teaching. Women in this church should therefore be encouraged to learn

in quietness and submission. They should not teach or take on positions of authority, lest the false teaching continue to spread. Eve, the first person ever to be deceived according to Genesis 3, provides a powerful warning for the churches in 2 Corinthians and 1 Timothy.

Conclusion

In this chapter, we have explored the vivid typologies used by the authors of Revelation, 2 Peter, 2 Corinthians, and 1 Timothy to warn their churches of the danger of false teaching, promise judgment on the false teachers, and encourage their churches to remain firmly within the teachings of the apostles. Beyond simple commands and prohibitions, the connections drawn with the famous deceivers and deceived of the Old Testament and Second Temple traditions place the church into the same story. The typologies make the danger of false teaching all the more terrible, and the reality of God's protection all the more secure.

PART TWO:

SOME EXAMPLES OF TRACING SCRIPTURE THROUGH SCRIPTURE

CHAPTER 8

THE REBELLIOUS SON: INTERPRETING AND REINTERPRETING A DIFFICULT TEXT

Caryn A. Reeder

Many, many parts of the Bible are quite difficult to understand: holy war in Joshua, rape and abuse in Judges and 2 Samuel, destructive punishment in Lamentations and Revelation. In one of these difficult texts, Deuteronomy 21:18-21, parents are instructed to take their disobedient, stubborn son to the elders of the city for judgment and execution by stoning.

For a modern reader, this law is beyond the pale. It has been labeled as child abuse, and described as draconian, cruel, and abhorrent. Ancient readers had similar reactions: should parents really have their child executed? In this chapter, we will explore the meaning of Deuteronomy 21:18-21 in its historical and literary contexts. Then, we will trace two paths of interpretation of this law in the Old Testament, New Testament, and Second Temple literature: one more literal, and one more metaphorical. The interpretation of Deuteronomy 21:18-21 in the ancient world can be a model for modern interpretations of troubling texts.

Deuteronomy 21:18-21

The law narrated in Deuteronomy 21:18-21 concerns a rebellious and stubborn son who does not listen to or obey his parents. The parents are instructed to accuse their son before the elders of the city as they sit in the gate, the place of local governance and judgment. The men of the city then execute the son by stoning him, so removing the "evil" from the midst of the people. (The son here, it should be noted, is likely a teenager or young adult, not a young child.)

This law demands a rather drastic response to a son's disobedience, a response that seems surprising in light of the importance of sons in Deuteronomy and its social context. Elsewhere in Deuteronomy, children are valued as signs of God's favor and heirs of the covenant (6:1-9; 11:18-21; 28:4 and 11). Children worship and sacrifice together with their families (5:14; 12:12, 18; and 16:11). Moreover, children would have been important in the agricultural society pictured in Deuteronomy.[43] All members of a household, from young to old, would need to work together in the home and fields for the family to survive. The household is the cornerstone of the community in Deuteronomy, and children are valued members of the family.

> Philo, Josephus, the early rabbis, and the New Testament authors lived under the laws of the Roman Empire. Only the Romans had the legal right to execute wrongdoers. The law of Deuteronomy 21:18-21 could not legally be enacted in Jewish or Christian communities under Roman rule.

The significance of children in Deuteronomy makes the law of the disobedient son not only more shocking, but also comprehensible. A son should be working on behalf of the household, supporting his parents, and maintaining the family's inheritance and land. He should be taking his place as a faithful member of the covenant community. Instead, the son of Deuteronomy 21:18-21 is rebellious and stubborn, and refuses to heed his parents. He is not learning to live by the covenant, nor is he accepting his role as a provider for the household. He is a danger to the community. To protect the rest of the community, the evil—the son—must be "purged."

The execution of the son reflects the danger of the situation. The entire community is threatened, and so the entire community joins in

---

[43] Note the repeated references to harvest (Deuteronomy 14:22-29; 16:9-10; etc.); the laws concerning fields, vineyards, and livestock (22:1-4; 23:24-25); the assumption that people will be out and about in the fields (21:1; 22:25); etc.

punishing the son for his refusal to be faithful to the covenant. However, while we may be able to understand the reason for the son's execution within Deuteronomy, the law remains a disturbing text. Ancient interpretations of the law in the Old Testament, New Testament, and Second Temple literature can provide a model for our own interpretation. In general, early interpretations of Deuteronomy 21:18-21 take the text in two different directions: first, literal interpretations that provide instructions for child rearing or examples of disobedience, and second, metaphorical interpretations that make the son a representative of Israel. These interpretations distance themselves from the violence of the law, providing ancient and modern readers with alternatives to execution.

Literal Interpretations of the Rebellious Son

Some ancient interpretations remain within the primary meaning and significance of the law of the rebellious son in Deuteronomy. These interpretations include the instructions for child rearing in Proverbs, the commentaries of Philo and the early rabbis, and the examples of disobedient sons in Josephus's books and the New Testament.

One way to deal with a potential rebellious son is to teach him to be obedient. In Proverbs, key words and themes of Deuteronomy 21:18-21 are incorporated into instructions for raising wise, obedient sons. Proverbs and Deuteronomy have a very similar theology.[44] Notably, as in Deuteronomy 21:18-21, sons in Proverbs are expected to be obedient, honorable members of the community (see especially Proverbs 23:20-21, 28:7). To this end, Proverbs offers many instructions for raising and disciplining sons.

Unlike Deuteronomy, however, in Proverbs the danger of a rebellious, stubborn son is met not by stoning, but by instruction. Chapters 1 through 7 address sons directly, calling them to live wisely according to the teachings of their parents and of God (1:8-9, 3:11-12). Later in the book, parents are told to teach or discipline their sons while there is hope.

---

[44] Compare, for instance, Deuteronomy 6:6-9 with Proverbs 6:20-23 and 7:1-5, or Deuteronomy 4:40 and 5:16 with Proverbs 3:1-2 and 9:10-11.

Parents are not to desire their destruction (19:18).[45] In Proverbs 23:13-14, beating a son will save him from Sheol. These texts use some of the same words and ideas as Deuteronomy 21:18-21, but their aim is not execution. Rather, when parents teach and discipline their sons properly, the sons become honorable, wise members of the community who need not be stoned for disobedience.

The interpretation of Deuteronomy 21:18-21 in Philo's commentaries follows a similar trajectory. Philo, a Jewish theologian in Alexandria, wrote commentaries and interpretations of the first five books of the Bible. In *On the Special Laws* 2.232, he works through the law step-by-step, explaining the motivation of the law and how precisely the parents should deal with their children (for Philo, young sons and daughters are in mind; Spec. Laws 2.227, 232). According to Philo, the parents are the gods of the household, and just as a person owes God obedience, so children owe their parents obedience (Spec. Laws 2.225-230). Parents in turn have the right to discipline their children with words, beating, physical restriction, and even death if the children are "carried away by their incorrigible depravity"

If either of [the parents] was maimed in the hand, or lame or dumb or blind or deaf, [the son] cannot be condemned as a stubborn and rebellious son, for it is written, 'Then shall his father and his mother lay hold on him'—so they were not maimed in the hand; 'and bring him out'—so they were not lame; 'and they shall say'—so they were not dumb; 'this is our son'—so they were not blind; 'he will not obey our voice'—so they were not deaf.

m. Sanh. 8.4

Herbert Danby. The Mishnah: Translated from the Hebrew with Introduction and Brief Explanatory Notes Oxford: (Oxford University Press.) 1933.

---

[45] In Hebrew, discipline and instruction are the same word, and it is not always clear which meaning is intended in a particular text. In effect, the two meanings overlap: to teach is to discipline (Proverbs 5:12, 10:17, etc.).

(232).46 Philo understands that this end is extreme. He says that it takes excessive wrongdoing to overcome parental love and justify execution. But Philo is also convinced of the necessity of such an end, if the child's behavior is so wicked. Such a child is an enemy of all people, and to protect the larger community, the child must be sacrificed (248). Philo's careful exegesis of the law, and also his comments on the extremity of the law, are developed much further by the early rabbis. The rabbis of the second and third centuries are famous for their very precise interpretation and expansion of the law of Moses. In the case of Deuteronomy 21:18-21, the rabbis surround the law with so many requirements that it becomes impossible to execute a rebellious son.

According to *Mishnah Sanhedrin* 8.1-4, the son's age is limited to very early puberty. He must eat a certain amount of meat and drink a certain amount of Italian wine; the meat and wine must be stolen from his father but eaten outside his father's home. Both parents, in perfect health and soundness of body (see sidebar), must condemn their son after repeated appearances before judges. In case all the requirements are met, the rabbis offer a final loophole: the son can run away to escape execution.

According to *patria potestas*, Roman fathers had the right to put to death members of their household. For wives and daughters, this right was generally restricted to sexual misconduct; for sons, the right was exercised in cases of political rebellion. The case of Herod the Great's sons would fall under this category. As a Roman ruler, Herod could exercise his right to execute his sons under *patria potestas*.

The rabbis do see a reason for the law in Deuteronomy. The disobedient son is condemned because he is a danger to himself and the world (8.5). However, their commentary on the law reveals their general disfavor for the law, and in effect silences the law. In fact, later rabbinic

---

46 *Philo*. 1927-62. Translated by F. H. Colson, G. H. Whittaker, and R. Marcus. 10 vols. (+ 2 suppl.). Loeb Classical Library (Cambridge, MA: Harvard University Press).

commentary on *Mishnah Sanhedrin* claims that "there has never been, and there never will be, a rebellious and incorrigible son" (*t. Sanh.* 11:6).[47]

Biblical traditions bear out this comment. Not one rebellious son in the Old Testament faces the punishment of Deuteronomy 21:18-21 (see, for instance, 1 Samuel 2:12-17 or 2 Samuel 13:21). There are very few examples of such punishment outside the Old Testament, either. Josephus, a Jewish historian in the first century, tells of Herod the Great's use of Deuteronomy 21:18-21 and Roman traditions of *patria potestas* to put to death two of his own sons (*Jewish War* 1.536-543 and *Jewish Antiquities* 16.356-369), but Josephus clearly disapproves of Herod's actions (note *Ant.* 16.362-363).

The absence of biblical stories of the execution of stubborn, rebellious sons suggests that the use of Deuteronomy 21:18-21 was limited. This conclusion is borne out by the discomfort with the law expressed by Philo and the rabbis. The appearance of key words and themes from Deuteronomy 21:18-21 in Proverbs' instructions for child rearing provides a very different use for the law: not to execute, but to raise children who will not be subject to the law. If parents instruct and discipline their children well, then their children will not need to be executed. These traditions remain within a literal interpretation of Deuteronomy 21:18-21, but it is a literal interpretation that turns away from execution towards education and discipline.

The Rebellious Son as Metaphor

The metaphorical interpretation of Deuteronomy 21:18-21 makes the son into a type of rebellious, stubborn Israel. This metaphor is part of Deuteronomy itself: God disciplines Israel as a man disciplines his son

---

[47] Jacob Neusner. The Tosefta: Translated from the Hebrew with a New Introduction. 2 vols. (Peabody, MA: Hendrickson, 2002).

(8:5), but rather than listening to God, Israel rebels (9:23-24, 31:27). The son and Israel are alike in their disobedience, and like the son Israel will face punishment and destruction (28:15-68,;32:19-29). Unlike the son, though, for Israel there is hope of future restoration (e.g., 32:36-43).

> Jesus is apparently called a glutton and a drunk (Matthew 11:19 and Luke 7:34). The people of his hometown try to stone him to death (Luke 4:16-30), and his family tries to take control of him because they think he has lost his mind (Mark 3:21). These hints suggest that Jesus could have been seen as a disobedient son, a charge his lifestyle would support: abandoning his family, challenging Jewish tradition.

The typology of the rebellious son is developed much further in the prophets, where Israel and the Israelites are repeatedly described as a stubborn and rebellious people who refuse to listen to or obey God (Isaiah 63:8-10; Jeremiah 5:23; Ezekiel 2:3-8; Hosea 4:16; etc.). In Isaiah 30, Israel is indicted as stubborn sons who seek the help of Egypt rather than obeying God (vv. 1-2). The prophet is told to write this message in a book as a witness against the people (v. 8): "For these are rebellious people, deceitful children, children unwilling to listen to the LORD's instruction" (v. 9). They seek to leave the way of God (v. 11), and their disobedience will lead only to destruction. But as in Deuteronomy, Isaiah also promises restoration. God will again be gracious and instruct the people, teaching them the proper "way" to live (v. 21).

The hope for the restoration of rebellious Israel is not part of the law of the rebellious son in Deuteronomy 21:18-21, but the typology does provide an alternative to the son's execution and absolute destruction. The New Testament offers another alternative. In 1 Corinthians 5:13, Paul quotes a refrain found in several laws in Deuteronomy: "expel the wicked person from among you." Considering the sexual nature of the wrongdoing in view in this chapter, Paul may be thinking primarily of the laws of Deuteronomy 22:13-25. However, there is also reference to drunkenness in 1 Corinthians 5:11, and chapter 4 ends with an extended comparison of the church with a rebellious child. These factors suggest Deuteronomy 21:18-21 may also be in mind in 1 Corinthians 5:13.

The identification of the church as rebellious son is also found in Hebrews. While Deuteronomy 21:18-21 is not explicitly referenced, in Hebrews 3-6, the church is warned against rebelling as Israel did in the wilderness. In Hebrews 12:5-11, the church is identified as the child of God, disciplined by God to be holy and righteous. The church should accept this discipline for their own good. Here the metaphorical and real intertwine: the church should behave like a good child who accepts parental instruction and discipline.

Like good children, they should imitate their father— just as Timothy, a "beloved and faithful" son, imitates Paul (1 Corinthians 4:16-17).[48] However, the Corinthians are not good children. They are arrogant against Paul. He offers them a choice: he will come to them either with love and gentleness or with a rod of discipline (1 Corinthians 4:21, as in Proverbs 10:13; 26:3; etc.). The identification of the church as a misbehaving child, refusing the father's instruction, echoes Deuteronomy 21:18-21. However, instead of executing his rebellious children in the church, Paul encourages the expulsion of wrongdoers from the church. His faithful children should not associate with them; they should be turned away, perhaps in hopes of their eventual restoration (1 Corinthians 5:5; 2 Corinthians 2:7-8).[49]

The hope for the restoration of a rebellious son is also present in Luke 15:11-32. The parable of the prodigal son does not explicitly cite Deuteronomy 21:18-21, but it does tell the story of a grown-up son who rebels against his father to indulge in drunken dissipation. The father would have every right to severely discipline his son, and certainly both

---

[48] As texts like Sirach 30:1-13 and John 8:39-44 indicate, sons were (ideally) reflections of a father's character and occupation.
[49] Compare Matthew 18:15-22.

Jewish and Roman societies would expect the father to punish such behavior. Instead, the father accedes to the demands of the son, and when the son returns, penniless and shamed, restores him to life as a son of the household. New Testament scholar N. T. Wright sees in this parable an allegory of Israel, who went into exile for rebellion against God, their father, and then were restored.[50] This connection suggests that Luke 15:11-32 is a layered metaphor: the rebellious son of Deuteronomy 21:18-21 provides a typology for Israel's rebellion against God, a typology that is re-embodied in Jesus' story of a rebellious son—and the father's forgiveness in the parable thus implicitly offers an alternative to the execution of the rebellious son in Deuteronomy 21:18-21.

These metaphorical rewritings of the rebellious son do not apply the law to actual children. Rather, they extend the story of the son to Israel and the church. The typology is not exact. Unlike the rebellious son of Deuteronomy, the punishment of Israel and the church is not absolute; Israel and the church can be forgiven and restored. This possibility, though, can affect our interpretation of Deuteronomy 21:18-21. The typology of Israel and the church as rebellious son offers a different ending for the law.

Reinterpreting the Rebellious Son

These examples show the different ways in which a single text, the law of Deuteronomy 21:18-21, was interpreted in antiquity. The same law led to detailed commentaries on how the law should (or should not) be carried out, instructions for child rearing, metaphors of rebellion, and promises of forgiveness.

Some of the interpretations identify the intent of the law in Deuteronomy as the encouragement of effective child rearing practices. For Proverbs and Philo, proper instruction of children means that a parent would never need to make use of the law of Deuteronomy 21:18-21. The more metaphorical interpretations of the law expand it into the story of a people who refuse to listen to or obey God, instead going their own way.

---

[50] See N. T. Wright, *The Challenge of Jesus* (London: SPCK, 2001), 24.

Like the son, the people will suffer—exile in the case of Israel in Isaiah, or expulsion from the community in the case of the rebellious Corinthians. But this story, unlike the story of the son, could have a happy ending. If in their exile the people remember God and return to the covenant, they will be restored. If Paul's rebellious children repent they can be saved. If the prodigal returns, the father will forgive. These retellings of the story rewrite the ending.

This exploration of the biblical and Second Temple uses of Deuteronomy 21:18-21 offers two important lessons on biblical interpretation. First, while we sometimes want to find one single, persistent meaning for a text, ancient readers and writers were comfortable with multiple meanings for the same text. The Bible itself witnesses to the use and reuse of a text in situations that recognize its original context and intent, and in situations that reapply the language of the text to a different end. As modern readers, we cannot ignore the original context of a text— this context helps us, so far removed from the biblical worlds, to understand the Bible. But we also should not ignore the multiple meanings given to a single text by later readers.

Second, the example of the rebellious son also shows us how very important it is to be familiar with the Bible. The authors of the Bible were well aware of earlier texts. They weave references, words, and ideas into their own works, and when we recognize these references, our understanding is deepened. Intertextuality is fun, enlightening, and key to our interpretation of biblical texts.

CHAPTER 9

WHO IS THE SUFFERING SERVANT?

Beth M. Stovell

Some passages in the Old Testament have been so used in the New Testament that Christians often are unaware of how those Old Testament passages were read prior to the New Testament. This is the case with the figure of the Suffering Servant in Isaiah and other parts of the Old Testament. This chapter asks the question, "Who is the Suffering Servant?" We will answer this question by examining the Suffering Servant in Isaiah and then by studying the Suffering Servant in the New Testament.

Starting with the time of the exile, the Old Testament frequently fers to a common of a righteous figure who suffers on behalf of others. This righteous

Examples of these suffering servant passages in the Old Testament include passages in Isaiah 40-55, Zechariah 1:15; 12:9-14; 13:6-8; and many of the Psalms.1

figure is described as "the Suffering Servant" because the term "servant" is frequently used of this figure.

This chapter will focus on the passages in Isaiah 40-55 that are referred to as the "Servant Songs". These are the most extensive sources describing the Suffering Servant figure in the Old Testament.

In the past many have assumed that Jesus is the Suffering Servant in the Old Testament. We see this in the early Church Fathers who spoke of Isaiah as "the fifth gospel" because of its significance for understanding the other four gospels and the identity of Jesus. [51] Yet the depiction of the Suffering Servant in Isaiah when read within Isaiah's historical context and

---

[51] John F. A. Sawyer, *The Fifth Gospel: Isaiah in the History of Christianity* (Cambridge University Press, 1996), 1-20.

read in its place in Isaiah 40-55 presents a more complex picture of the uffering Servant than if we simply begin by identifying this figure with Jesus from the start.

Our interpretation of the Suffering Servant is connected to our understanding of how typology works. Typology occurs when something in the Old Testament becomes a prototype for something in the New Testament. A typology is only realized after the type is established in the second text. For example, in the Old Testament, God's presence dwelt with the people in the form of a tabernacle, a movable tent where the Israelite people worshipped. The tabernacle was later replaced with the temple as the locus of God's presence. In John's Gospel, the language of "tabernacle" is used to describe Jesus coming in a physical body (John 1:14 "The Word became flesh and tabernacled among us") and John explains that Jesus is referring to his body when Jesus says that he will rebuild this temple in 3 days (John 2:20-21). John is creating a typology between the tabernacle/temple of the Old Testament and Jesus in the New Testament, but this typology can only be realized when we read John. People in Old Testament times did not generally expect the tabernacle or temple to be a reference to a future person, but the disciples saw this connection because of their experience with Jesus. Similarly, the Servant Songs had their own original meaning within Isaiah that becomes a valuable typology in the New Testament for the understanding of early believers as to why Jesus had to die and what it meant to their lives and the lives of future generations.

> Isaiah's role as the "fifth gospel" has not only impacted the New Testament, but has impacted art, music, and literature through the centuries. This can be seen in musical works like Handel's *Messiah*, commentaries of the early Church Fathers, and William Blake's poetry. See John F. A. Sawyer, *The Fifth Gospel: Isaiah in the History of Christianity* (Cambridge University Press, 1996), 1-20.

Isaiah 40-55: Suffering Servant Songs

The Servant Songs are located in a section of passages in what is commonly referred to as "Second Isaiah." While the first section of Isaiah 1-39 appears to be dated largely the 8th century during the invasion of the Assyrian empire, the second section of Isaiah 40-55 marks a noticeable shift in terms of situation. This second section of Isaiah (or "Second Isaiah") speaks to the situation of the Israelites who have now been taken into captivity in Babylon. This exile from their homeland deeply impacts the Israelite people. This experience of suffering and loss makes the people begin to ask why God

The theme of the temple is a vital one throughout the Old Testament and the New. This theme impacts ideas about God's dwelling place and how we understand God's mission in relation to the Church. Greg Beale explores a biblical theology of temple from the Old Testament to the New in his work, *The Temple and the Church's Mission: A Biblical Theology of the Dwelling Place of God.* New Studies in Biblical Theology (Downers Grove, IL: InterVarsity Press, 2004).

could allow such a situation to occur. How could the Israelites be the people chosen by God and yet God could allow them to be taken away from their land and placed into slavery under foreign rulers? Understanding the situation of the exile has an impact on the Suffering Servant figure in Isaiah. It is from these questions that the story of the Suffering Servant arises as a means by which God, through his prophet, explains why this suffering has happened to Israel and gives them hope in the midst of this suffering.

The Suffering Servant is described in four passages commonly called the "Servant Songs": Isaiah 42:1–4; Isaiah 49:1–6; 50:4–9; 52:13–53:12. These Servant Songs describe the Suffering Servant in two different ways. At times the Suffering Servant appears to be an individual, representing a righteous sufferer, and at other times the Suffering Servant appears to be communal, representing Israel as a group. To provide examples of these two types of depictions, we will examine the Servant

97

Songs and demonstrate where this tension lies in the portrayal of the Servant.

To understand the description of the Suffering Servant in Isaiah 42, many believe it must be read in light of Isaiah 41's description of God's servant. In Isaiah 41, God repeatedly describes Israel as his servant. Isaiah 41:8 states, "But you, Israel, my servant, Jacob, whom I have chosen," and Isa 41:9 states, "I took you from the ends of the earth, from its farthest corners I called you. I said, 'You are my servant'; I have chosen you and have not rejected you." Read in this light we might expect the Servant to be a communal character representing Israel, but Isaiah 42 seems to shift some of this usage.

Isaiah 42:1–4 begins its designation and description of the role of the Suffering Servant using the title "servant" and "my chosen one" in Isa 42:1. Both are titles used of David elsewhere. Isaiah 42:1 also describes this Servant's role as "bringing justice to the nations." Isaiah 42:2–3 further characterizes the Servant and his task. In v. 2, the Servant is characterized by his silence. Verse 3 describes the Servant as a bruised reed not broken and "a faint wick" that is not "extinguished" to explain how the Servant brings forth this justice. This justice becomes described in terms of faithfulness in the second half of v. 3. Carol Dempsey suggests "the servant's mission is not only to the victims of injustice but also to the perpetrators of injustice. Both groups are bruised reeds and smoldering wicks."[52] Isa 42:4 uses the same verbs associated with light and nature in v. 3 to describe the steadfast commitment to this Servant's task of justice, and the verse extends this justice and the Servant's teaching to the whole earth. Thus, Isaiah 42's depiction of the Suffering Servant tends to describe this Servant in individual terms as one who seeks justice in the midst of his persecution and for the sake of other victims of injustice.[53] Yet when we read further in Isaiah 42, the individual aspect of the servant appears to

---

[52] Carol Dempsey, *Isaiah: God's Poet of Light* (Danvers, MA: Chalice Press, 2010), 144.

[53] Hanson notes the universality of this scope by noting the parallel structure between "justice to the nations" and "justice on the earth". See Paul D. Hanson, *Isaiah 40-66*, Interpretation Bible Commentary (Louisville, KY: Westminster/John Knox Pr, 1996), 42.

change into a more communal understanding of servant. In Isaiah 42:19, after a passage directed at Israel, Yahweh describes Israel as a blind servant. In this verse, the Servant appears to be Israel as a whole. Isaiah 43–45 and 48 continue this communal description of Israel as the Servant in Isaiah 43:10. Israel is called the Lord's witnesses and his chosen servant. Isaiah 44:1; 44:2; 44:21; 45:4; and 48:20 each describe either Jacob or Israel as "my servant."

A similar tension between the individual and communal characteristics of the Servant figure occurs in Isaiah 49. In fact, in Isaiah 49 it sounds as if Isaiah the prophet (or the author of Second Isaiah) is described as the Servant. The prophet states, "Before I was born the LORD called me; from my birth he has made mention of my name (Isaiah 49:1)" and "He said to me, "You are my servant, Israel, in whom I will display my splendor (Isaiah 49:3)" and "And now the LORD says—he who formed me in the womb to be his servant to bring Jacob back to him and gather Israel to himself... (Isaiah 49:5)." However, in v. 3 this Servant is referred to as Israel. Isaiah 49:6 notes that this Servant will not only come to re-gather Israel, but also to bring salvation to the world: "I will also make you a light for the Gentiles, that my salvation may reach to the ends of the earth." Again, it is unclear whether this is the action of an individual who represents Israel, Israel as a community, or specifically of the prophet, Isaiah.

Similar to Isaiah 49, Isaiah 50's depiction makes it sounds likely the Servant is the prophet, Isaiah. This comes from phrases like, "The Sovereign LORD has given me an instructed tongue, to know the word that sustains the weary." The prophet's job as

> It is common within Biblical Hebrew poetry to find frequent shifts between the subject of sentences that make it hard at times to determine who is doing a particular action. This is obvious in Isaiah 49, but it is also found frequently in the Psalms and in other prophetic literature.

messenger of God's word is an important theme in both Isaiah 49 and 50. This is found in Isaiah 50:10 asking who listens to the word of the Lord's

Servant. Yet this also creates an overlap with the discussion of Israel as God's messenger to the world that we find in Isaiah 42:19. This Servant is described as experiencing mocking and spitting (v. 6) and having accusers against him (v. 8), but receiving vindication from God in the end.

Isaiah 53's depiction of the Suffering Servant begins in Isaiah 52:13.[54] Most scholars see these two passages as connected. Determining whether the Suffering Servant in Isaiah 53 is communal Israel or an individual is a matter of great debate in Christian and Jewish circles. While most Jewish scholars would argue that Isaiah 53 is identifying Israel as the Suffering Servant, many Christian scholars identify this Suffering Servant as an individual in this passage.[55] There are logical reasons for either of these interpretations. Those seeing Isaiah 53 as about the community of Israel highlight that the theme of Isaiah 52:1-12 leading up to the Suffering Servant passage focus on the redemption of Israel. Further, the verses in Isaiah 54 following Isaiah 53:12 (the end of the Servant Song) return to the theme of Israel's redemption. They also point to the many passages that explicitly describe the servant as Israel. Those who argue that Isaiah 53 describes an individual (likely not the prophet Isaiah due to the use of "we" in vv. 4–6) point to the request for Israel to look upon him (52:13), the description of the Suffering Servant as "a man of sorrows" (53:3), and how the suffering put upon him creates peace and healing for the prophet and Israel (53:4-6).

The depiction of the Suffering Servant in Isaiah 53 integrates several key elements from the accounts of the other Servant Songs. The Suffering Servant is "rejected...despised" and abused (53:3; cf. 49:7; 50:6); the Servant's suffering becomes a sacrificial payment for the sins of the people (53:4–6, 12; cf. 42:3–4); the Servant is brought to the lowest depths,

---

[54] For more discussion of the Suffering Servant in Isaiah 53 and its history of interpretation, see Bernd Janowski and Peter Stuhlmacher, eds., *The Suffering Servant: Isaiah 53 in Jewish and Christian Sources* (Grand Rapids: Eerdmans, 2004).

[55] However, it should be noted that not all Christian biblical scholars see the Suffering Servant of Isaiah 53 as individual. There are many who argue that while Isaiah 53 is originally about a communal Israel, it is then read typologically in the New Testament as an individual.

even to death (53:8–9, 12); but ultimately the Servant is redeemed and lifted up to sit with kings (53:10–12; cf. 49:7) and will redeem the nations (53:12; cf. 42:1–6; 49:6). As we will see below, these elements are picked up by the New Testament authors in their reflections on Jesus as the Suffering Servant.

In order to understand the significance of the role of the suffering servant in Isaiah, we must return to the struggles faced during the exile. During the exile, many of the people were taken from their homes and relocated to Babylon where they were enslaved. Due to this exile, the people experienced homelessness, a loss of identity, humiliation, and enslavement. This experience was one of great loss and suffering. It is not surprising then that in the writings from the time of the exile, the people asked the questions, "Why are we experiencing this suffering and loss? Why did God desert us?" The prophecy of the Suffering Servant provides answers to these questions by showing that there is meaning to the people's suffering and their loss. Through the Suffering Servant, God shows that He is present with the people, knows their suffering and loss, and will ultimately restore them. This restoration occurred through the words of the prophet, who thus functioned as a Servant to God. Yet this restoration also came through the faithfulness of a remnant of the Israelite people, who thus also functioned as God's Servant. This remnant and the prophet both suffered despite being righteous before God, thus creating the theme of the righteous one who suffered for others. Both the remnant and the prophet as the Servant are described as being restored and redeemed, instilling hope into the hearts of the audience of the book of Isaiah.

Jesus as the Suffering Servant in the New Testament

The story of the Suffering Servant continued to speak to the Jewish people throughout their generations and into the time of the New Testament in the 1st century. The Suffering Servant figure that began in Isaiah is found in later prophets like Zechariah and in the Psalms. By the time of the New Testament, the Jewish people were under the rule of foreign powers yet again: this time, Rome. In this midst of their continuing experiences of loss, the New Testament writers saw Jesus as the ultimate and typological fulfillment of the Suffering Servant story.

In Mark's Gospel, Mark develops a theme that connects Jesus' self-description as the Son of Man to the Suffering Servant in Isaiah. While in the original context for the Son of Man in Daniel 7, the Son of Man is not depicted in terms of an experience of suffering, Mark's addition of Isaiah throughout his Gospel allows for connections between the experience of the Son of Man, who will be glorified beside the

> Daniel 7:13-14 (NIV): "In my vision at night I looked, and there before me was one like a son of man, coming with the clouds of heaven. He approached the Ancient of Days and was led into his presence. He was given authority, glory and sovereign power; all nations and peoples of every language worshiped him. His dominion is an everlasting dominion that will not pass away, and his kingdom is one that will never be destroyed."

Father, and of God's servant who must experience suffering to redeem others. Mark seems to be able to make this connection by focusing on the downward and upward movement that occurs to the Suffering Servant in Isaiah. The Suffering Servant is brought down to the depths, even to death, and brought back again to the high places by God. This allows Mark to draw a similar connection to the Son of Man in Daniel 7. The Son of Man can only reach his location beside God (as depicted in Dan 7), if he first, like the Suffering Servant, goes down into the depths of suffering and death. In this way, the Son of Man's life becomes a "ransom for many" (Mark 10:45).[56]

Like Isaiah 42, in Matthew 12:18 Jesus is declared God's servant, whom he has chosen. God puts his spirit on him and he will bring justice to the nations. In Matthew 20:24-28 it is Jesus as this servant who becomes

---

[56] For further discussion of this relationship between the Son of Man and the Suffering Servant in Isaiah, see Francis Moloney, "Excursus 2: Son of Man and the Suffering Servant in Mark 10:45" in Moloney, *Mark: Storyteller, Interpreter, and Evangelist* (Peabody, MA: Hendricksen, 2004), 213-14.

the model for the servant of all who must suffer. Matthew's focus on discipleship encourages all of Jesus' disciples (including us!) to follow his example of servanthood to the point of being persecuted like Jesus.[57] In this way the Suffering Servant in Matthew has both an individual and communal aspect to its depiction.

Acts 8:26-40 tells the story of Philip's encounter with an Ethiopian eunuch and his explanation of the Suffering Servant passage in Isaiah 53:7–8. Called by an angel of the Lord, Philip finds an Ethiopian eunuch reading Isaiah. The eunuch wants to know "who the prophet is talking about, himself or someone else?" Acts 8:34 explains that Philip starts with Isaiah 53:7–8 and "told him the good news about Jesus." As noted above, the eunuch's question about whether the Suffering Servant is the prophet or someone else demonstrates that he has experienced the same tension in reading the passage that we described above. This tension likely existed because the eunuch was reading the Suffering Servant passages together and trying to understand the identity of the Suffering Servant. Philip provides an answer to the eunuch that includes a description of Jesus, seemingly as the Suffering Servant. Questions arise about Philip's way of interpreting the Old Testament. Is Philip saying to the eunuch that Jesus *is* the Suffering Servant of Isaiah 53:7–8 or is Philip explaining the Suffering Servant as a prototype for Jesus? The answer to this first question is not clearly provided by the text of Acts. A secondary question is whether we are able to follow the same steps that Philip took in interpreting Old Testament passages.

Examining these New Testament uses of Isaiah's Suffering Servant we find certain shared elements. In their own way, each of the New Testament authors sees Jesus as typologically fulfilling the vision found in Isaiah. Mark focuses on the necessity of suffering of Jesus to complete his redemption of others and his own glorification. Matthew extends Isaiah's vision from Jesus to Jesus' disciples, seeing them as an

---

[57] Persecution and discipleship is a theme found throughout Matthew. James D. G Dunn, *Jesus' Call to Discipleship*, Understanding Jesus Today (Cambridge: Cambridge University Press, 1992), 116–117.

extension of Israel as communal servant. In Acts, Philip suggests that reading about Isaiah's Suffering Servant provides a means for extending Jesus' mission to the nations (in a similar way as the Suffering Servant provided the Lord's salvation to the nations). Thus, each of the New Testament authors is highlighting different aspects of Isaiah's original vision to help their own community.

Conclusion

When we approach Isaiah's Suffering Servant only through the lens of Jesus Christ first, we miss the potential power of understanding the role of the Suffering Servant in its location within the exile experience. Understanding the situation of the exile provides a backdrop to the experience of suffering and the question "Where is God?" that then echoes in the New Testament. One of the most common issues facing modern Christians and non-Christians alike is how we wrestle with suffering and loss in the world today. The story of the Suffering Servant shows us that God consistently redeems suffering and loss, not by giving us lives where suffering never happens, but by allowing us the walk through the suffering and come out on the other side stronger and refined. God gave this hope and promise to the Israelite people in the time of the exile and shared that same message with them in an even deeper and richer way through the experience of God coming to dwell with them in the person of Jesus. When we see Jesus as the Suffering Servant in light of the exile experience, we see Jesus' crucifixion and resurrection as part of God's continuing pattern for the world: though we walk through suffering and even death, we come out reborn and resurrected. God is able to do something greater with us than we ever imagined on the other side of the suffering.

Setting Jesus up as the Suffering Servant connects Jesus to the story of Israel as the Suffering Servant. As described in Ch 5: Hearing God's Prophets, Jesus is understood by the New Testament authors as the fulfillment of faithful Israel promised in the Old Testament. To connect Jesus to the story of the Suffering Servant is to link Jesus to the story of Israel. As the Suffering Servant, Jesus takes on the communal role as well as the individual role, representing Israel in its experience of loss and suffering. In his death, Jesus reaches to the lowest places, even into a darker place than the exile itself. Yet Jesus' story remains in continuity with the Suffering Servant's story as his death is redeemed in the resurrection.

This means that Jesus' story as God's Suffering Servant is more than just a story about his humility and innocence, or even about Jesus' forgiving our sins, but also an answer to the question of suffering itself: In our darkness places, when we feel the most exiled from God, God is still working out his plans through those who will remain true to God even in the midst of their suffering. This suffering leads to resurrection and fullness: as it did for the Suffering Servant in Isaiah and as it did in the life of Jesus, it continues to happen in our lives today.

Part Three:

Reading Scripture Well

Chapter 10

What Not to Do with those Amalekites — and Other Ways to Abuse Scripture

Ralph K. Hawkins

In Chapter 2, we considered how the authors of the biblical books use intertextuality to tell the story of God redeeming his people. We used the book of Joshua as a test case, and saw that its author appropriated themes from the Pentateuch in order to tell the story of the Israelite conquest of Canaan. Just as the author of Joshua looked back and appropriated previous traditions, so later biblical authors looked back to the book of Joshua to tell the story of God's ongoing redemptive activity. Significantly, we saw that later biblical authors quote selectively from Joshua, leaving out references to specific battles and human activity, and making God the sole actor. In the intertestamental period, the author of 1 Maccabees appropriated the person of Joshua typologically in order to justify Judas Maccabeus' leadership of the Jewish rebellion. New Testament writers understand Jesus to be the perfect antitype of Joshua, but stress that the "rest" anticipated by the Israelites will only be fulfilled when God finally and climactically establishes his kingdom.

Among the authors of Scripture, therefore, the conquest was seen as a unique, one-time event in which God acted on Israel's behalf. While some Jews in the intertestamental period certainly saw the Jewish revolt as a sort of reenactment of the conquest, the authors of the New Testament believed that the "rest" promised in the Pentateuch and sought in the conquest would only be experienced at the end-time, when Jesus fully establishes his kingdom. Many centuries after the New Testament, some Christian interpreters of the Bible, however, appropriated the conquest traditions typologically and used them as justification for colonialism and

109

genocide. In this chapter, we will look at select examples of this typological usage, discuss why they are inappropriate, and discuss alternatives to typological appropriation.

Using the Conquest Traditions to Justify Genocide

In the book of Genesis, God promised Abraham that he would give the land of Canaan to his descendants (Genesis 15:18-21). However, he was told that they could not inherit it for four hundred years, because "the sin of the Amorites [had] not yet reached its full measure" (Genesis 15:13-16). As time passed, however, the native population apparently persisted in their sin until they had reached a "point of no return," practicing child sacrifice, sodomy, bestiality and other vices (Leviticus 18:21, 25, 27-30). God gave the Israelites the command to implement a "ban" against them, which comes from a Hebrew word with a root idea of setting aside or devoting something for a special purpose. In the Bible, when the ban is used in military contexts, the NIV translates it as to "devote" the enemy to God through destruction. For example, when the Israelites attacked Jericho, the text relates, "they devoted the city to the Lord" (Joshua 6:21). The instructions about the ban in Deuteronomy included the command to utterly destroy all the men, women, and children belonging to the seven Canaanite nations (7:1-2). They were to be cut off to prevent the corruption of Israel (20:16-18), who was going to be given the land in their place.

When the Israelites left Egypt in order to undertake the journey to the Promised Land, a Bedouin tribe called the Amalekites attacked them in the Sinai Desert and came under God's judgment (Exodus 17:8-16). Moses told the Israelites that, "when the Lord your God has given you rest from all your enemies on every hand, in the land that the Lord your God is giving you as an inheritance to possess, you shall blot out the remembrance of Amalek from under heaven; do not forget" (Deuteronomy 25:19 NRSV). When Israel had settled in the land, and Samuel had anointed Saul as the nation's first king, he charged the new monarch with the task of completing the annihilation of the Amalekites:

Samuel said to Saul, "I am the one the Lord sent to anoint you king over his people Israel; so listen now to the message from the Lord. This is what the Lord Almighty says: 'I will punish the Amalekites for what they did to Israel when they waylaid them as they came up from Egypt.' Now go, attack the Amalekites and totally destroy all that belongs to them. Do not spare them; put to death men and women, children and infants, cattle and sheep, camels and donkeys" (1 Samuel 15:1-3).

Throughout the history of the church, people have sometimes tragically turned to these conquest traditions to justify war and colonialism. Examples of this abound but, for the sake of brevity, I will mention just a few.

When Pope Urban II launched the first Crusade in A.D. 1095, he told the army that "it is our duty to pray, yours to fight against the Amalekites."[58] The Crusade movements in the high Middle Ages and late Middle Ages frequently invoked scripture for justification. This is evident in papal Crusade proclamations, in Crusade sermons, in historiographical reports, in charters and letters of those who participated, in Crusade poetry, and in numerous contemporaneous visual illustrations of the Crusades.[59] Among the biblical texts appropriated to justify the Crusades were those concerned with the exodus theme and those focused on holy war. Palestine was praised as the Promised Land and, as such, worth the difficult journey and the challenges involved in taking it militarily (as in Genesis 15:1-21; Exodus 3:8). Likewise, the Muslims were the antitype of the heathen occupants of Canaan who deserved God's wrath.[60]

---

[58] Elliot Horowitz, *Reckless Rites: Purim and the Legacy of Jewish Violence* (Princeton: Princeton University Press, 2006), 120-21.

[59] See the bibliography for Stefan Tebruck, "Crusades, Crusader," in *EBR* 5:1117-18.

[60] This description is not intended as a political statement about the Crusades, but simply to show how those who participated in the Crusades used Scripture. Muslim accounts of the first Crusades present the incursions from the West as a brutal, unprovoked onslaught over which the Muslims eventually triumphed. This portrayal, however, has been brought into question in Rodney Stark, *God's Battalions: The Case for the Crusades* (New York: HarperOne, 2009).

The Protestant Reformation produced religious conflict that often led to violence, which the participants often justified on the basis of the conquest traditions. For example, the Swiss reformer Heinrich Bullinger (1504-1575) postulated a special class of warfare modeled on the conquest traditions that could be initiated "upon men who are incurable, whom the very judgment of the Lord condemneth and biddeth to kill without pity or mercy. Such were the wars which Moses had with the Midianites, and [Joshua] with the Amalekites … [these are] the wars that are taken in hand for the defense of true religion against idolators and enemies of the true and catholic faith."[61]

A number of Puritan writers in the early 17th century developed theories of war based on the doctrine of the ban, some of whom specifically quote from the book of Joshua.[62] Oliver Cromwell (1599-1658), who experienced a religious conversion in the 1630s and became an independent Puritan, entered the English Civil War and quickly rose through the ranks to become a key commander. He saw himself as a sort of Puritan Moses, and he drew parallels between his own revolution and the exodus.[63] On the basis of this comparison, Cromwell viewed Irish Catholics as "Canaanites," and believed that, like the ancient Israelites, he and his soldiers were exempt from the common rules of morality in seeking to annihilate them.[64]

Throughout American history, there has been a tradition of reference to and comparison with ancient Israel, the chosen people, and the idea of the Promised Land. The American Puritans saw themselves as having been chosen by God to establish the American Israel. Clear analogies were persistently made between the Pilgrims and the Israelites. Explicit examples of this include Increase Mather's *The Day of Trouble is*

---

[61] Thomas Harding, *The Decades of Henry Bullinger.* 2 volumes (Charleston, Nabu, 2010), 376-77.

[62] For examples, see James Turner Johnson, *Ideology, Reason, and the Limitations of War: Religious and Secular Concepts, 1200-1740* (Princeton: Princeton University Press, 1975), 118-33.

[63] Michael Walzer, *Exodus and Revolution* (New York: Basic Books, 1984), 3-4.

[64] Roland H. Bainton, Christian Attitudes Toward War and Peace: A Historical Survey and Critical Re-Evaluation (Nashville: Abingdon Press, 1960),151.

Near[65] and Cotton Mather's *Magnalia Christi Americana.*[66] In this latter work, Mather specifically described William Bradford, the governor of Plymouth Colony, as "a Moses," "the leader of a People in the Wilderness," and New England as a wilderness Jerusalem. Just as Puritan settlers were interpreted as antitypes of biblical figures, so Native Americans were identified as Canaanites or Amalekites who warranted punishment and destruction. For example, in the midst of a series of conflicts in the 1680s that led to significant losses by New Englanders, Cotton Mather (1663-1728) preached a sermon on September 1, 1689, entitled "Soldiers counseled and comforted: a Discourse delivered unto some of the forces engaged in the late war of New England against the northern and eastern Indians." In it, he gave the soldiers this assurance: "It is the war of the Lord which you are engaged in, and it is the help of the Lord that we are at home affectionately imploring for you."[67] Mather understood the colonists to be the antitype of the Israelites and the Native Americans the antitype of the Amalekites. He encouraged the colonists to fight against "Amalek annoying this Israel in the wilderness."[68] The colonial preacher Robert Gray expressed the hope that the Indians might convert but, if they did not, he believed that the biblical commands were clear, by which he meant the command to implement the ban against the Canannites.[69] Some years later, Herbert Gibbs thanked God for having extirpated "the enemies of Israel in Canaan," by which he meant the Native Americans who occupied the New Promised Land.[70]

The identification of Americans as a chosen people and their land as a Promised Land continued throughout American history and is

---

[65] Increase Mather, *The Day of Trouble is Near* (Cambridge, MA.: Marmaduke Johnson, 1674).

[66] Cotton Mather, *Magnalia Christi Americana* (Hartford: Silia Andrus & Sons, 1855).

[67] Abijah Perkins Marvin, *The Life and Times of Cotton Mather* (Charleston: BiblioLife, 2009), 84.

[68] Alfred E. Cave, "Canaanites in a Promised Land: The American Indian and the Providential Theory of Empire," *American Indian Quarterly* 12.4 (1988), 286.

[69] Ibid.

[70] Ibid.

expressed in the term "manifest destiny," which became a popular slogan in the nineteenth century. According to this doctrine, just as Joshua had outlined the territorial allotments for the twelve tribes of Israel (Joshua 13-21), so God had established the boundaries of the United States for the American people.[71] Just as Joshua had urged the Israelites to settle the whole land of Canaan, so the doctrine of Manifest Destiny saw the American settlers as entitled to expand over the whole Promised Continent, driving out any "Canaanites" who opposed them.[72]

The typological appropriation of the exodus and conquest traditions is certainly not unique to American history. There are many other examples of such tragic misuse of these Scriptural traditions. The Boers of South Africa interpreted their experience under British rule through the lens of the exodus traditions.[73] Explorers, settlers, and missionaries in Australia saw themselves as similar to the Israelites as they settled in Canaan, and genocide against Australia's indigenous inhabitants was carried out on the basis of the conquest traditions.[74] Israeli nationalists have contended that present-day land seizures are scripturally grounded and that antipathy and rigor toward the inhabitants of those lands has scriptural warrant.[75] Other examples could be cited, but we must turn to the question of how we can set limits on this kind of appropriation of biblical traditions.

---

[71] Stephen A. Douglas, Congressional Session of January 31, 1845. Cited in Steven Grosby, *Biblical Ideas of Nationality: Ancient and Modern* (Winona Lake, IN: Eisenbrauns, 2002), 224, n. 20.

[72] See the essays in Part 3 in Conrad Cherry, *God's New Israel: Religious Interpretations of American Destiny* (Englewood Cliffs, NJ: Prentice-Hall, 1971), 111-53.

[73] Walzer, Exodus and Revolution, 11-12.

[74] Roland Boer, *Last Stop Before Antarctica: The Bible and Postcolonialism in Australia* (Atlanta: Society of Biblical Literature, 2008), ch. 3; Mark G. Brett, *Decolonizing God: The Bible in the Tides of Empire* (Sheffield: Sheffield Phoenix Press, 2009).

[75] Moshe Greenberg, "On the Political Use of the Bible in Modern Israel: An Engaged Critique." Pp. 461-71 in Pomegranates and Golden Bells: Studies in Biblical, Jewish, and Near Eastern Ritual, Law, and Literature in Honor of Jacob Milgrom. Edited by David P. Wright, David Noel Freedman, and Avi Hurvitz (Winona Lake, IN: Eisenbrauns, 1995).

Appropriating the Conquest Traditions

The key issue in appropriating the conquest traditions is violence. Because of the divinely sanctioned violence in the book of Joshua, many interpreters have shied away from a literal reading and have sought other strategies for interpreting it. In this section, we will review some of the ways these traditions were appropriated by New Testament authors, as well as some cases of their usage in the history of the church. Finally, I will suggest some interpretive guidelines for modern readers.

New Testament Appropriation

The primary method by which New Testament authors appropriated material from the exodus-conquest traditions was typological. For example, Ananias and Sapphira are antitypes of Achan and his family (Joshua 7:16-26; Acts 5:1-11). Their stories serve a similar function, since each appears at the beginning of a new covenant. In Jude v. 5, the author writes that, "Though you already know all this, I want to remind you that the Lord delivered his people out of Egypt, but later destroyed those who did not believe." The author of the book of Revelation probably understood Jesus as the antitype of the commander of the Lord's army (Joshua 5:13-15; Revelation 19:11-16) and the inheritance of the land of Canaan in the book of Joshua as a type of the renewed heavens and earth (Joshua 13-21; Revelation 21:1-2).

I am hesitant about the possibility that Christian readers today can use typological methods of interpretation. The authors of the New Testament used this method in reading the exodus-conquest traditions, but we believe they were guided by inspiration, which prevented them from misapplying the traditions. Even in the patristic period, the church fathers established firm boundaries for this approach. They taught that: (1) the literal sense of the text under question should not be abolished; (2) there should be a correspondence between the historical fact and the proposed spiritual idea, and (3) those two readings should be apprehended together.[76]

Church History

In church history, the allegorical method predominated. For example, in his sermons on the book of Joshua, Origen (died c. A.D. 253) argues that the book does refer to historical facts, but that it should be read primarily as a story of Christ's salvation of humankind. Augustine (died A.D. 430) believed that the Scriptures contained four levels of interpretation, including (1) eternal truths; (2) narrated facts; (3) predicted future events; and (4) precepts. While this left room for varied interpretations, he did insist on some guidelines. He insisted that a viable interpretation had to correspond with the teachings of the church and promote love for God and others. If the literal interpretation of a text did not yield a reading that promoted love, then it must be understood figuratively. Augustine did not see how to read the passages in Joshua that describe the annihilation of the Canaanites at the hand of God in these ways, and so he became convinced that they had no literal meaning and could only be understood allegorically.

Jerome (347-420), on the other hand, insisted on identifying the original meaning, and this approach burgeoned in the Reformation with Martin Luther's (1483-1546) focus on the grammatical, historical meaning. Evangelicals have tended to focus on a grammatical-historical method to the exclusion of any kind of allegorical or other approach that seeks a "deeper meaning."[77] Some biblical scholars have eschewed the existence of a "deeper meaning" in the biblical text, while others have argued in favor of it. In a classic study, Raymond Brown argued that there may be a "deeper meaning" in Scripture that God intended but that the human

---

[76] J. N D. Kelly, *Early Christian Doctrines*. Revised edition (San Francisco: HarperSanFrancisco, 1978), 76.

[77] See the Chicago Statement on Biblical Hermeneutics, which can be found online at http://library.dts.edu/Pages/TL/Special/ICBI_2.pdf.

author was not aware of, and that such a meaning might be brought out through an allegorical approach.[78]

Reading Strategies for Today

How can we read the exodus-conquest traditions today? And, importantly, how can we read them in ways that do not perpetuate violence? I propose six guidelines.

First, I would stress that believers should avoid reading Scripture alone, by which I mean that it should not be read in isolation from the believing community of the church. Christians must read the Scriptures with an awareness of how they have been read and interpreted in the historic church. Reading the biblical text in this way can at least provide some safeguards against novel or far-fetched interpretations.

Second, specific Old Testament texts cannot be read in isolation from the rest of Scripture, but must be read in their canonical context. Regardless of what book or passage we are reading, we must read "across the canon" to see how it fits into the overarching story of what God has done.

Third, the conquest traditions should be read according to the standard canons of interpretation of historical narrative, including attention to the narrator's point-of-view, the scenes that make up the story and how they relate to one another, the characters, dialogue, plot, and features of structure.[79] It has become fashionable today to urge readers of the book of Joshua to read it from the perspective of the Canaanites, an approach that is designed to take today's readers out of the role of "conqueror" and enable us to identify with the "victims" in the story.[80]

---

[78] Raymond E. Brown, *The Sensus Plenior of Sacred Scripture* (Baltimore, MD: St. Mary's University Press, 1955).

[79] See Gordon Fee and Douglas Stuart, *Reading the Bible for All It's Worth*. 3rd edition (Grand Rapids, MI: Zondervan, 2003), 93-99.

[80] E.g., Royce M. Victor, "Reading Joshua as a Canaanite." Pp. 90-91 in *Global Perspectives on the Old Testament*. Edited by Mark Roncace and Joseph Weaver (Boston: Pearson, 2014), 90-91.

This approach, however, is fraught with interpretive mistakes that lead us away from the true meaning of the text. By taking it out of its context, we assume that its purpose is to provide morals for living. By supposing that it applies to us, we redefine its meaning because we are not satisfied with what it appears to say. The fallacy of this approach is that it ignores the fact that the story of the conquest was not written to provide modern readers with an example to be followed or morals for living, but to show the progress of God's history of redemption.

Fourth, there is no warrant in the New Testament for continuing the wars of the conquest. The word Amalekite does not even occur in the New Testament, and the term Canaanite only occurs once, when Jesus shows compassion to a Canaanite woman (Matthew 15:21-28). The conquest was a one-time event by which God simultaneously punished the Canaanites and established the Israelites in their land. Once that had occurred, it did not need to be repeated again. In fact, in the New Covenant, God's people do not have an earthly country that is "their land," but belong instead to a heavenly one (Hebrews 11:16).

Fifth, Christian readers should interpret the conquest traditions in light of the cross. The conquest was not completed during the time of Joshua, nor in subsequent Old Testament history, but finds its ultimate fulfillment in the work of Christ. When the seventy whom Jesus had sent out returned after having gone "to every town" preaching the arrival of the Kingdom of God, Jesus said that, as they conducted their preaching, he watched Satan "fall like lightning from heaven" (Luke 10:17-18). Paul explains that Jesus "disarmed the powers and authorities, he made a public spectacle of them, triumphing over them by the cross" (Colossians 2:15).

Sixth, the New Testament derives a "deeper meaning" from the conquest narratives that it then applies to the Christian life. A clear example of this is that the work of Jesus in conquering the world is continued through his followers. After he had been crucified, buried and raised, Jesus appeared to his disciples and gave them a final charge. He told them, "you will receive power when the Holy Spirit comes on you; and you will be my witnesses in Jerusalem, and in all Judea and

Samaria, and to the ends of the earth" (Acts 1:8). This might be taken as an echo of the conquest traditions. Jesus said that believers would "receive power" when the Holy Spirit came upon them for their task, which was going to involve witnessing for him in Jerusalem first and then spreading out to "the ends of the earth." Just as the early Israelites were to settle the entirety of the land of Canaan, so the witness of Jesus' followers would result in measurable, geographical growth. That growth would begin in Jerusalem, spread throughout other Jewish areas to areas on the fringes of Judaism, and finally to "the ends of the earth." Jesus' followers may conquer the world on his behalf, but it is to take place through witnessing, evangelism, and discipleship rather than through literal warfare.

There is also a sense in which Christians are called to engage in warfare, but it is spiritual rather than literal. Paul calls Christians to

Put on the full armor of God so that you can take your stand against the devil's schemes. For our struggle is not against flesh and blood, but against the rulers, against the authorities, against the powers of this dark world and against the spiritual forces of evil in the heavenly realms. Therefore put on the full armor of God, so that when the day of evil comes, you may be able to stand your ground, and after you have done everything, to stand. Stand firm then, with the belt of truth buckled around your waist, with the breastplate of righteousness in place, and with your feet fitted with the readiness that comes from the gospel of peace. In addition to all this, take up the shield of faith, with which you can extinguish all the flaming arrows of the evil one. Take the helmet of salvation and the sword of the Spirit, which is the word of God. And pray in the Spirit on all occasions with all kinds of prayers and requests. With this in mind, be alert and always keep on praying for all the saints (Ephesians 6:10-18).

Obviously, the battle envisioned by the apostle here is one against the Devil's schemes. The "full armor" is of a divine nature, and the only piece of offensive weaponry listed is the "sword," which symbolizes the Word of God. The Gospel proclaimed by the Christian soldier is a Gospel of peace. With all this having been said, one can only conclude that those who would appropriate Scripture violently are taking it out of context for their own use.

CHAPTER 11

PLEASE TRY THIS AT HOME: STEPS FOR READING SCRIPTURE DEEPLY

Michael D. Matlock

At the core of this book, we have sought to demonstrate that Scripture can be understood and applied in even more fruitful ways when Bible students seek to understand how a writer of a biblical passage cites or alludes another biblical passage or uses typologies or allegories to communicate ideas that either fully constitute or strengthen the details of the passage. We have also endeavored to illustrate where understanding Second Temple Jewish texts also assist our understanding of the conversation that is occurring in the canonical dialogue of Scripture.

Before we discuss how to notice intertexture (particularly the kinds of intertextuality demonstrated in previous chapters) in a biblical or Second Temple Jewish text, there are some foundational steps to any healthy biblical interpretive approach. First, before interpreting a passage of Scripture, read, and if possible, make some preliminary survey notes of themes, motifs, and tropes. While we are on this subject, try to note recurrences of words or phrases, as well as contrasts, comparisons, cause-effect, effect-cause, introduction, and climax in the biblical book you are studying.[81] Second, raise some interpretive questions that are directed at the observations that have been made while reading a biblical book. There are three main types of questions: basic definitional or explanatory questions such as what does this observation mean? Who or what is

---

[81] Comments are meant to be suggestive. There are many other things any Bible student can do when reading completely through a biblical book at one time. See David Bauer and Robert Traina, *Inductive Bible Study: A Comprehensive Guide to the Practice of Hermeneutics* (Grand Rapids: Baker Academic, 2011), 79-142.

involved? How is this accomplished? And, when or where is this accomplished? There are rational questions designed to answer why something is included in the text. Finally, there are implicational questions raised to address the full implications of a particular thing with a particular meaning having been placed here for these particular reasons.

When a student of Scripture has decided on a passage to study within a biblical book, there are many steps to general interpretation and application that one could recommend. Offering specific step-by-step guidance to all interpretation is not the purpose of this chapter. Thus, again, I will simply mention a couple of suggestions before we delve into interpretation that involves intertexture or inner-biblical exegesis between texts.[82] First, pay careful attention to the literary contexts and the genre of the passage, which most often contain the most significant types of evidence for interpreting a passage of Scripture. As you study the nearby context, describe how the verses that immediately precede and follow the passage contribute to the ideas of the passage you are seeking to interpret. Then broaden your scope and look at the larger segment of the book where your passage is contained (e.g., if interpreting Matthew 5:43-47, look at what connects the specifics of this passage to the larger "Sermon on the Mount" in Matthew 5-7). Also, think back to your notes and observations from your survey of the entire book. Ask how this writer of this biblical book has fastened and united your passage to the larger book.

Next, determine the genre(s) of this passage and how this particular literary form should be interpreted. We interpret poetry differently than parable. We understand parable differently than apocalyptic texts. We decipher apocalyptic texts in a different manner than discursive or logical texts, and so on.83 Finally, as faithful interpreters of a biblical passage, seek to discover as much of the historical background of the passage as possible. We may need to discover historical background that pertains to the setting of the writing itself or the setting of persons, events, or things that are mentioned or alluded to within the book. We

---

[82] Again, see Bauer and Traina, *Inductive Bible Study*, 179-248, for more interpretation guidance.
[84] See Gordon Fee and Douglas Stuart, *How to Read the Bible For All Its Worth*, 4th ed. (Grand Rapids: Zondervan, 2014).

strongly urge all Bible students to have in their possession at least one standard Bible dictionary and to consult it often in interpretation.[84]

Up to this point, all steps described for interpretation have primarily been focused upon studying a passage of Scripture with a priority upon the immediate, segment, and book contexts of a passage.[85]

In this area of interpretation, the passage we are studying may make use of some type of inner-biblical exegesis or intertextuality. We turn our attention in the remainder of this chapter to the issue of guiding Bible students to be attentive to quotations, allusions, typologies, and allegories and to determine the significance of these intertextual connections.

> When we notice a possible quotation or allusion, look for both continuity and discontinuity between the older and updated texts and critically engage the conversation between the two or more texts. For example, when we begin studying the NT with Matthew, we should note the many quotations of the OT (there are 43) that the writer employs and ponder the purposes of the quotes.

Being Attentive to Quotations and Allusions

The preeminent form of intertextuality is when a writer quotes another passage of Scripture or Second Temple Jewish text by either citation or allusion. Lexical resemblances (or more generally "textual sameness") constitute a commonly agreed criterion by which to measure proposed inner-biblical allusions. There are two broader groups of quotation and allusion, explicit and implicit uses. For example, an explicit quotation is any verbal parallel of at least two words, which is explicitly

---

[85] See John Walton, et al, *The IVP Bible Background Commentary: Old Testament* (Downers Grove, IL: IVP Academic, 2000) and Craig Keener, *The IVP Bible Background Commentary: New Testament* (Downers Grove, IL: IVP Academic, 1994).
[86] A very useful resource for this step of Bible study is John Kohlenberger, *Zondervan NIV Naves's Topical Bible* (Grand Rapids: Zondervan, 1992).

identified by a quotation formula, or some marker.[86] Quoting from Isaiah 54:1, an example occurs in Galatians 4:27: "For it is written: 'Be glad, barren woman, you who never bore a child; shout for joy and cry aloud, you who were never in labor; because more are the children of the desolate woman than of her who has a husband.'" An explicit allusion entails a reference to a given text or a quotation formula in addition to which a given text is paraphrased or a keyword or theme of a given text is employed. Again in Galatians 4 (vv. 22-23; cf. v. 29), Paul alludes to Genesis 16:15 and 21:2, 9: "For it is written that Abraham had two sons, one by the slave woman and the other by the free woman. His son by the slave woman was born according to the flesh, but his son by the free woman was born as the result of a divine promise."

> We are not really finished with our interpretation of a passage until we have noted how our passage of study is conversing with other texts in Scripture and is often building upon earlier or contemporary biblical texts. It is imperative to note the same concepts and ideas in other passages.

On the other hand, implicit intertextures encompass implicit quotation, implicit allusion, implicit reference, reminiscence, and paratextual rewriting or expansion of a given text found in the OT. What makes an implicit quotation is something akin to any uninterrupted verbal parallel of at least three or four words that does not alter the quoted text but is not introduced by a quotation formula or otherwise explicitly identified. An implicit allusion involves a parallel of at least three or four words to another text. Thus, we read in Mark 10:6 an allusion to Genesis

---

[86] An explicit intertexture entails any of the following options: 1) a previously written text disclosing the current text it is employing and includes explicit quotation with a formula or marked reference such as "as it is written," 2) explicit reference to a previously written text without quoting that text, 3) explicit allusion, and 4) the continuous commentary on a given book of the OT. Continuous commentary is not found in any NT books but it is very common in Second Temple Jewish texts.

1:27 and/or 5:2: "But at the beginning of creation God made them male and female."

Quotations are usually not as difficult to observe as allusions. The following are seven questions that a reader of Scripture may ask to determine the validity of a possible allusion.[87] 1. Was the proposed source of the echo available to the author and/or their original readers? 2. How "loud" is the allusion; that is, how explicit and overt is it? 3. How often does the author cite or allude to the same text? 4. How well does the alleged echo fit into the line of argument of the passage in question? Does the proposed precursor text fit together with the point the author is making? 5. Could an author in fact have intended the alleged effect of any proposed allusion, and could contemporaneous readers have understood it? 6. Have other readers in the tradition heard the same allusions that we now think we hear? 7. Does the proposed intertextual reading illuminate the surrounding discourse and make some larger sense of the author's argument as a whole? Do we find ourselves saying, "Oh, so that is what the author meant"?

Being Attentive to Typologies

A typological interpretation occurs whenever a biblical text is drawing upon a prior biblical or Second Temple text in terms of a person or people group (e.g., priests), objects (e.g., temple), events (e.g., creation), and ideas (e.g., sacrifice) within a historical framework as prefiguring, corresponding, or symbolizing some aspect of God's future activity.

To get a further sense of typological interpretation, we might think in terms of the English word typical and its connotation of that which bears the imprint of some distinctive pattern of design, thought, and so on. In the NT, this activity particularly relates to Jesus' personhood, cult objects, and events.

---

[88] Questions are drawn from Richard Hays, *Echoes of Scripture in the Letters of Paul* (New Haven: Yale University, 1989).

Often the type is messianic and frequently related to the idea of salvation. The key indicators of typology include standard OT types, examples, or patterns that the NT writer explains in light of new antitypes. For instance, Jesus who is the greatest high priest is depicted as the antitype of the high priest in the Israelite religion; also Moses and his relationship with Torah (the first five books of the Bible) is a subject type for Jesus and his function in giving Torah.

Many instances of typology do include the element of foreshadowing. The initial instance in a correspondence is called the *type* and the fulfillment can be designated as the *antitype*. However, not every specific person, event, object, or idea in the OT is a foundation for a typological comparison. We should also never forget that even when a NT writer uses an aspect of an OT text for a typology, that OT text still maintains basic meaning and significance in the historical context of its original setting. If the original historical, literary, and theological nuances of the type in the OT are not carefully explored, the antitype in the NT will not be fully appreciated in terms of understanding or application for Christian living. Moreover, the student of the Bible will not have built the proper foundation for the typology to be understood accurately. I am reminded of the misguided comment that I recently heard; the stone Jacob used for a pillow at Bethel was a type of Christ functioning as the foundation stone of the church. This person had given very little, if any, consideration to the original historical, literary, and theological settings of

Genesis 28.

Here are a few steps that can help a Bible student identify and interpret typologies. First, determine the basic meaning of the type in its literary and historical contexts. Probe the type and go beyond a superficial description. The OT type and the later OT or NT antitype must be grounded in a real historical, existing thing or person, not on a fictitious narrative (cf. allegory below). Second, search for the employment of a specific type throughout the OT and NT, and note the

Other examples of types and antitypes include the twelve tribes of Israel and the twelve disciples of Jesus, wilderness wanderings of the Israelites and the wilderness experience of Jesus and his followers, as well as the first Adam or man and the second Adam or Jesus. For the purposes of application, Christ becomes a type for Christians.[1] In this regard, the NT antitype must not lose its anchoring in the OT and be interpreted as the experience of the self.

consistencies or inconsistencies with each use of the type. Third, do not expect the type and antitype to consider every theological topic; therefore, limit the topic to the features of the context. Fourth, synthesize your analysis of a type by noting how the type or pattern is used in various places across Scripture. Fifth, be sure that you are not seeing types everywhere in Scripture, and, even when you are sure of a typology, ensure that you are not forcing every point of the two entities.

It is important to recognize that typology can be found in the OT itself (without the use of NT texts) such as Isaiah's use of the original central exodus event in Exodus for the Jews who were in captivity in Babylon (Isaiah 43). And yet, as Christians read the NT, they must be expectant of typology that employs an OT type.

Being Attentive to Allegories

In distinction to typology that may be described as an analogy of events, an allegory pertains to an analogy of words. In other words, an allegory is concerned with the words from which it draws out a concealed theology. Allegories may be understood as an extended metaphor (as already indicated in the introduction). A metaphor works by using something in the physical world to explain something abstract and difficult to understand. In addition, an allegory may be developed with more complexity into a method of reading a passage of Scripture.

In this second understanding of allegory, the church fathers, and most notably Origen, went so far as to affirm that many things in the OT were mythical and fabulous, existing *only* to portray the deeper and spiritual truths in the NT. Church fathers who interpreted in this fashion were trained either directly or indirectly in the Alexandrian school of interpretation in Egypt. Unlike typology, this use of allegory affirms little of the reality of the historical events that are background for the texts. We might call this interpretive approach hyper-allegory in which every detail of the text must represent some other reality. To give you some flavor of this approach, let us consider Augustine's interpretation of the parable of the "Good Samaritan" (Luke 10:29-37).

Every detail in the parable conveys a deeper, more spiritual truth. The man is Adam; Jerusalem is the heavenly city of peace from which Adam fell; Jericho means moon and is Adam's mortality, and like the moon it waxes and wanes; and thieves embody the devil and his angels who stripped him of his mortality, persuaded him to sin, and left him half dead. The priest and Levite are the priesthood of the OT and could profit nothing for salvation; Samaritan means guardian and is the Lord Jesus himself; binding of the wounds manifests the restraint of sin; oil is comfort of good hope; and wine is the exhortation to work with fervent spirit. The beast is the flesh in which Christ chose to come to us, and being set upon the beast he is the incarnation of Christ; the inn is the church where travelers who return to their country are refreshed after pilgrimage; and the morrow/tomorrow is after the resurrection of the Lord.

The two denarii are either the two precepts of love or the promise of this life and the life to come. Finally, the inn keeper is the apostle Paul; the supererogatory payment ("if anything more is needed") is either Paul's counsel to celibacy or Paul's working with his hands lest he should be a burden to the weaker brothers when the gospel was new even though it was lawful for him to live by gospel means. Apparently Augustine could not settle on either the deeper spiritual meaning of the denarii or the supererogatory payment. Augustine's allegorical method of interpreting Scripture is contra-contextual and destroys the unity of the parable by finding the whole of salvation history in the parable itself; it leaves too much room for imagination and personal bias.

There are numerous allegories in Scripture. However, one of the few passages in Scripture explicitly identified as allegory is Paul's comparison of Sarah and Hagar in Galatians 4:21-31 which also includes other forms of intertextuality, citation and allusion with formula in 4:22, 27 as noted above. With this passage in mind, let us explore how the allegory works and its significance for interpreting Scripture more broadly. Paul's use of allegory indicates a contemporizing of historic events in the OT and does not divorce his total interpretation from these considerations. The following chart contains the elements of the contrasting covenants. Implicit contrasts are set in parenthesis.

> Although a certain amount of skill is needed to interpret an allegory, a developing Bible student will begin to notice comparisons and contrasts designed to lead us to a coherent interpretation of a passage.

The lives of Abraham's two wives and two sons represent two covenants:		
Mosaic Covenant	vs.	Abrahamic Covenant
Son's mother was a slave - (Ishmael)	v.22,28	Son's mother was a free woman - Isaac
Son born according to the flesh	v.23	Son born through a promise

Mother is from Mt. Sinai - Hagar	v.24	Mother is from (Mt. Zion) - (Sarah)
Mother bears children into slavery	v.24	(Mother bears children into freedom)
Present Jerusalem	v.25,26	Jerusalem above
Children of (flesh)	v.28	Children of promise
Son born according to the flesh	v.29	Son born according to the Spirit

Paul's use of allegory assumes his audience knew the historical background of the text. Additionally, Paul's use of allegory does at least regard historical and literary contexts as something meaningful as he notes elements from Genesis 16-18 and 21. Paul is not using allegory akin to the way Origen (or Philo) uses it, and his major point is to clarify what it means to be a Christian who lives by the Spirit.

What interpretive principles can we draw from this biblical example of allegory? First, allegory is a figure of speech or an interpretive method used in Scripture. Like typology, allegory relies heavily upon comparison and correspondence: words and ideas for allegory and event, persons, objects, and ideas for typology. Second, allegory cannot be divorced from the historical or literary contexts from which it is drawn. Third, an allegory is meant to be demonstrative and explanatory of a specific vein of truth. Paul in Galatians 4 is debunking the idea that full obedience to the Mosaic law is necessary for salvation, at least not in the manner that the Judaizers are asserting in Galatia. Fourth, allegory is comprised of a number of metaphorical expressions in which the meaning of one word is infused in another word or concept. Closely related is the fact that none of the figurative expressions are so obscure as to leave us without any other recourse but to find some hidden meaning. Fifth, an allegory will demonstrate something profitable and applicable for the Christian life.

Conclusion

We invite you now to (re)consider not only the importance of detecting intertextuality in the form of citation or allusion as well as typology or allegory, but also the benefit of unpacking these forms of intertextuality for understanding the historical, literary, and theological angles of Scripture. The steps outlined in this chapter should help guide us in this most important endeavor of understanding Scripture. Wherever an inner-biblical allusion or intertextuality occurs in Scripture, always be prepared to carefully observe how the earlier text amplifies the later text and also how the later text innovates the earlier text. A conversation is always happening among biblical texts. Not only should Christians pay attention to the conversation that is occurring between these two or more texts, but we should also pay attention to the entire metanarrative of redemptive history in the process.

Chapter 12
Conclusion

E. Randolph Richards

As an adolescent, I picked up the Bible and found life-changing treasure within its pages. As I grew and matured, I understood more of the Bible and of life and thus drew even more from the riches of Scripture. This book, though, has encouraged me to go farther, to seek additional vantage points from which to read God's Word in order to gain even more. When we notice how one biblical author cites another, linking two or more parts of Scripture, we see the deeper connections that the author intended, for those who have "ears to hear," as Jesus said about those able to see the link between John the Baptist and Elijah (Matthew 11:7-14). When Luke quotes a part of Psalm 2, where God's enemies conspire against the Lord's Anointed, Luke wants—even expects—his readers to look at all the other ways that Psalm 2 applies to the story of Jesus. When we miss those other connections, we miss treasures that Luke hoped we would see. The book of Joshua used key words to link the reader back to Deuteronomy. So also, later Old Testament books, and even New Testament books, likewise use key terms and phrases to hook their stories back to what God has been doing all along. The authors expected us as readers to notice these links, to appreciate that God has one united story and to uncover deeper insights from these intertextual connections. ` Instead of quoting a passage, a biblical author may allude to or just hint at another older story, expecting us to pick up on the connection. Scholars sometimes call these hints intertextual echoes. While Christians today are often quite familiar with Psalm 51 (as a prayer of repentance), Jesus' hearers knew another prayer of repentance just as well (or perhaps even better), the Prayer of Manasseh. When Jesus told his parable of a repentant tax collector, many of his

133

hearers would recall this other, older, story of an infamous sinner who humbled himself and repented. If God could forgive Manasseh, surely a tax collector had hope of forgiveness. Why? Because they knew God was "the God of those who repent" (Pr Man 13).

Another even less direct way to connect stories requires readers to know Scripture well. A biblical writer could tell an allegory, expecting the hearer to remember that such an allegory had been used previously in another book. Christians today are often quite familiar with Jesus' allegory in John 15, that he is the vine and we are the branches. We may not, though, have linked that back to Isaiah's allegory of the vine. By understanding the deep richness of Isaiah's image, we can appreciate even more how, when Jesus stated his father was the vine gardener, he had picked a metaphor his hearers already knew. This wasn't the first time God has been described this way. When Jesus told his disciples they are part of the vine, they were not surprised. They were a part of Israel and Israel had previously been described as a vine. The threat of judgment was also an expected part of the story. But Jesus' disciples were told they could avoid being the part of Israel that was judged (pruned and discarded). How could the disciples avoid the fate that befell Israel in Isaiah's day? By abiding in Christ, because he is the true Israel that bears fruit—the good fruit, unlike the Israel of Isaiah's day. Thus, we saw that reading John 15 intertextually (connecting it) with Isaiah 5 enabled us to read Jesus' allegory more deeply.

A parent of rowdy teenagers may on occasion be a tad sympathetic about Deuteronomy 21 and its instructions for dealing with a stubborn and rebellious son. Nonetheless, no matter how exasperating a teenage child might be, no sane Christian parent would even dream of escorting her child to the elders for execution. Are we then just to shrug off this passage, dismissing it? Should we take out our scissors and expunge it from the pages of our pew Bibles? Do Christians just say, "Thank God it is in the Old Testament!" and then ignore it? Caryn Reeder shows us that this temptation (to find a way to dismiss or negate the passage) was how later Jewish leaders were handling Deuteronomy 21. Rather, she helps us to see how Jesus taught us to deal with "a son who does not listen to or obey his parents." We are to wait like the father in Luke 15. If the son returns, we are to forgive the repentant son. Although I have read profitably Jesus' parable of the Prodigal Son for years, this deeper reading of Scripture opened my eyes to additional blessings from this story.

Reading Scripture deeply carries us often into typology, an area many modern readers find bewildering, but typology can help the discerning reader to see more. Joseph Dodson assisted us by explaining the New Testament intended us to think typologically, that is, to notice "Jesus reminds me of Isaac" or "Jesus is like Adam" or "Jesus is greater than David." These earlier characters created a type or pattern that Jesus repeated, often in deeper, fuller or broader ways. Typology wasn't just limited to Jesus. Matthew prepares us for Mary's scandalous story by linking her to other biblical women whose own stories had questionable elements but whom God pronounced righteous. Although typology is one of the more subtle ways to read Scripture deeply, it can be one of the most rewarding.

For the reader who has ears to hear, a biblical writer may build upon a pattern he has seen, a typology, guiding us to connect across books, even testaments. We often say that a pattern can reveal a habit or even character. When we see a pattern of how God acts, perhaps we even glimpse into the heart of God. Or, a pattern can help us to see a subtle implication. In Genesis, we read that God descends to confuse the tongues of men. Even in humanity's fallen state, with one language "nothing they plan to do will be impossible for them" (Genesis 11:6). The pattern of acting, this "type," seen at Babel, is repeated at Pentecost. This time, though in a reversal, the confusion of multiple languages is overcome by God again descending. Is Luke implying the same conclusion: "nothing they plan to do will be impossible for them"? This time, though, the conclusion is about the church as the Kingdom of God advancing in this world, where even the gates of Hell cannot stop it.

Typology is so subtle and so easy to overlook. So why did the biblical authors bother to use it? Because typology can be a very powerful motivator. Let's use an illustration. The Revelation has letters to churches in seven towns in Asia Minor. Imagine in one of those towns a woman owned a bakery, one that had been in her family for generations. When she became a Christian, she removed the statue of Fornax (the Roman goddess of baking) from the niche in the sidewall of her shop. Her neighbors and fellow bakery shop owners were more than merely shocked. When our young Christian refused to contribute toward the cost or even to participate in the Fornacalia, the festival in Fornax's honor on February 17, her fellow bakers were outraged. Wasn't she risking the wrath of Fornax, who might burn down all their bakeries? How could she endanger them all like that? Did she no longer love her fellow bakers? These bakers might even pressure the barley sellers to boycott her until she came to her senses. Our new Christian baker would experience intense social pressure to "add" the worship of Jesus without stopping visits to the other temples. Reeder reminded us of the role that temples had in everyday life. The struggle of our young Christian baker would be exacerbated by (false) Christian teachers like the Nicolaitans who were teaching that it was okay to visit the other temples. How could John help a new believer like her to withstand such pressures? One way was the use of typology. By describing these false teachers with certain phrases, the readers of the Revelation were expected to exclaim, "Oh my, these leaders remind me of Balaam and Jezebel." Typologies carry extra power. Those who knew the story of Balaam felt horror and shame over how the Israelites fell into sexual sin and idolatry through Balaam. This emotional freight gets carried over with the Balaam story to those leaders. Typology isn't meant just to inform but to vividly motivate us. It was felt in the gut and not just thought in the head.

Paul mentioned that Eve was deceived because she was created second. She was more easily deceived <u>not</u> because she was female but because she had heard the commands of God secondhand (via another human, Adam). Although Adam had directly heard God give the command, Eve only heard it from Adam. Thus Eve isn't a type or an example of women but an example, a type, of <u>all</u> of us Christians.[88] We didn't hear Jesus give the Sermon on the Mount in Galilee; rather, we hear it secondhand from Matthew. We didn't see Jesus raise Lazarus from the dead; we rely on the testimony of John. Our faith is based not upon our

---

[88] Actually Eve represents humanity (male and female) in other ways as well. Adam was made from dust, while Eve came from another human (Adam). So also all of us come out of another human (our mothers).

own eyes but the faithful testimony of others. So like Eve, we must guard ourselves from being deceived by false teachers,[89] who prey upon our weakness. Like the original serpent, they question whether our source of information was reliable. As the serpent suggested that Eve should doubt Adam's word ("Did God really say…?"), so we should guard against false teachers who suggest we should doubt that our sources are trustworthy. When I note "These false teachers remind me of the Serpent in the Garden," suddenly I <u>feel</u> the danger as well as know it.

Reading Scripture deeply, seeing the intertextual connections, often requires us, though, to know not just the stories in our Old and New Testaments but also the popular versions of the biblical stories circulating at the time. These are found in documents scholars call Second Temple literature. Reeder mentions the audience for letters like Jude and 2 Peter were influenced by Second Temple writings like 1 Enoch. These writings were often retellings or elaborations of biblical stories. While most of us have never heard of them, these were the "Bible stories" many Jews grew up hearing. Let's consider another example: 1 Peter using these Second Temple stories. When encouraging wives, 1 Peter describes Sarah "who obeyed Abraham and called him her lord" (1 Peter 3:6). In the Genesis account, the stories of Sarah may not necessarily conjure up images of wifely submission. In Genesis, she does not call him "lord." Yet, in the Second Temple story, *The Testament of Abraham,* Sarah is quite obedient and calls Abraham "my lord" five times. Before we object, is it really so odd that someone would know a popular retelling of a biblical story better than the original biblical story? Most of my students know the story of Noah and the flood, not from Genesis 6 but from a movie or from Vacation Bible School. When I ask them why God flooded the earth, they respond it was because mankind was wicked. They do not seem to know the more specific reason cited in Genesis 6:1-5 about the sons of God having sex with the daughters of men. In fact, they look scandalized and don't believe

---

[89] The young widows of 1 Timothy may well have been wealthy patronesses. Their influential social stands and finances may have been what attracted the false teachers to them. New believers of financial means (whether male or female) would do well to heed Paul's warnings.

me until they look in Genesis. So, likewise Peter makes his point about wifely submission by using the stories of Abraham his audience knew.

Ralph Hawkins reminds us of the horrors inflicted upon humanity in the name of Christ by those who misuse the story of Joshua and the conquest of Canaan. He then suggests how we might better understand those stories as showing the progress of God's history of redemption and not as a pattern to emulate. Michael Matlock then continues this theme of how to use a deeper reading of Scripture. When we understand better how Scripture cites or alludes to itself, how it connects one part to another through allegory or typology, we uncover intertextual richness.

Most students of the Bible are aware that "context matters." We are to look at the verses before and after the passage we are studying. We even know we are to look at the larger context of the book or letter. Yet, we have also seen that our biblical writers often expected us to reach across books, even across the canon, to see more subtle connections. Sometimes it was a bit more obvious, like when Paul compares the New Covenant to the story of Abraham's two sons, or when the Ethiopian Eunuch calls our attention to the connection between the Servant of the Lord and Jesus. Yet, other times this intertextuality is less obvious, such as when John connected Jesus to Wisdom,[90] who was standing by God's side as he created (Proverbs 8:27-31), or Jesus' parable of the prodigal son as a better method than stoning to deal with a stubborn and rebellious son. While a simple straightforward reading of Scripture has always and continues to impact and change lives, this book has challenged us, when we are ready, to move beyond drinking milk to eat more solid spiritual food (1 Corinthians 3:1-2).

---

[90] John connects Jesus with Wisdom in several other ways as well; see E. Randolph Richards, "Signs of the Restoration," in *The Story of Israel: a Biblical Theology*, ed. Marvin Pate, pp. 153-176 (Downers Grove: InterVarsity Press, 2004), esp. pp. 165-66.

Made in the USA
Columbia, SC
26 August 2018